Critical Reflections

Previous Books:

Exposed to Winds
[Selected poems]

Construction Delay Claims
[Performance measurements]

Anecdotes of Would-be Experts
[Business experiences]

Thoughts in a Maze
[Various mysteries]

Trials and Errors
[Life experiences]

Characters
[A tribute to past friends]

Oddities
[False assumptions]

Connections
[Human beliefs & behaviors]

Conclusions Volumes I & II
[Reaching conclusions – right or wrong]

My Best Dog Days
[Autobiographical sketches]

Investment Fundamentals

Our Support Systems

About My Books

Human Traits & Follies

Honesty's Travesty

Critical Reflections

by

Arthur O.R. Thormann

Specfab Industries Ltd.

Edmonton, Alberta

2016

Library and Archives Canada Cataloguing in Publication

Thormann, Arthur O. R. (Arthur Otto Rudolf), 1934-, author
    Critical reflections / by Arthur O.R. Thormann.

ISBN 978-0-9916849-6-0 (paperback)

    1. Love. 2. Hate. I. Title.

BF575.T53 2016   152.4'1   C2016-905231-1

Copyright © Arthur O.R. Thormann, 2016

Publisher: Specfab Industries Ltd.
                  13559 - 123A Avenue
                  Edmonton, Alberta, Canada
                  T5L 2Z1
                  Telephone: 780-454-6396

Publication assistance by

PAGEMASTER
PUBLISHING
PageMaster.ca

Cover Designs: Front: Figure of a reflecting naked woman
                  Back: Symbol and text by author

How improbable is it
to love thy enemy?
Improbable enough
that most of us
won't even try,
thus ending
in hate!

♠

"Love Thy Enemy!"

♥

I dedicate this book to my friend James D.
Lampard

My gratitude goes to my daughter Nancy,
and to my friend Pam Sigvaldason,
for their valued advice.
All mistakes remaining are entirely mine.

Preface

I renamed my first version of *Conclusions Volume III* to *Human Traits & Follies*, and I renamed the second version to *Critical Reflections*. These two titles better define the contents of the books. However, I am still planning to write a third volume of *Conclusions*.

The notion of love kept recurring to me as a worthwhile topic. I was obsessed by the idea that love is everywhere, even where hate exists, because people who hate simply *love* to hate. Therefore, I decided to write about love and hate relationships. Can you think of a better topic for the main reason of our existence? Without love, we may as well not exist, because we would be no better off than a plant in the field, although plant lovers claim that plants also flourish more with love from them.

I have previously covered the subject *love against hate* in my book *Thoughts in a Maze*, so I won't repeat myself. Suppose we take the Bible instruction, "Thou shalt love thy neighbor as thyself" (Lev 19:18); what, exactly, does it mean? Some folks may not love themselves at all, in which case the instruction to love their neighbors as themselves may not mean much. Another instruction from the Bible, "Love ye your enemies …" (Lk 6:35), is also hard to imagine, especially when trying to love vicious lions and deadly viruses.

Enemies, bad neighbors, or unloving spouses, it is hard to love any of them in the biblical sense, but whoever can accomplish it is better off.

Love definitely causes different juices to flow in our bodies than hate. I would not be at all surprised to find out how many sicknesses can be traced to feelings of hate; conversely, I would not be at all surprised to find out how many sicknesses were healed by feelings of love. Those who find they are unable to love should, at least, try to neutralize their feelings of hate.

The topic of love literally provides an author limitless material for a book, as my readers will soon realize, since many of our experiences are founded in love/hate relationships. Yet, since the concept of love is manifold, the material available for a book is also manifold.

While writing such a book, the question arises: what is the greatest and purest form of love known to us? I believe it is the love that Jesus Christ spoke of and demonstrated to us on the cross at Golgotha; also, it could be the love that God decided to bestow on us, by allowing His beloved Son to suffer and die for us. But we will probably seldom be able to give such love to our enemies, especially to the vicious or deadly kind of enemies.

Again, I have used and, give credit to, the Wikipedia, to assure the accuracy of most historical inclusions. For the front cover, I chose a sculpture of a naked woman, to depict the exposed love of human beings, and to emphasize that we leave as naked as we came.[*]

Arthur O.R. Thormann
July 2016

---

[*] See Ecclesiastes 5:15

Contents

Introduction

Love and hate are opposite concepts. However, this does not mean that if one does not love something or someone one must hate it, him, or her. I talked one day with a friend of mine about people's favorite meats for Christmas. He said, "I love turkey." I said, "I love goose." The fact is, I don't *love* turkey, but I don't *hate* it either. If I'm invited for Christmas dinner and the hostess serves turkey, I will eat it.

There is a big area between love and hate – various degrees, as it were. One can almost love something or almost hate it, or neither love nor hate it. Very seldom do we just love or hate something or someone. One such example involves God and Satan. One can love God and hate Satan, there is seldom an in-between. The examples chosen for this book must be judged accordingly.

Take US President Barack Obama and Israeli Prime Minister Benjamin Netanyahu: Netanyahu, I think, made a political mistake accepting an invitation from John Boehner, the 2015 Speaker of the United States House of Representatives, to speak to Congress without notifying the White House. This was a slap in the face to Obama. Netanyahu aimed to stop Obama's negotiations with Iran regarding a nuclear agreement. After Netanyahu made his speech to Congress, assuring Congress that he had the highest respect for Obama, Obama said, in an interview with the media, that his negotiations cannot be criticized until finished, and, at that time, he will convince the American people of its wisdom. As it happened, Netanyahu did not accomplish to stop negotiations; he only accomplished making an enemy of Obama. On the other hand, Obama proved, by his response in the media interview, that he is the more astute politician.

Where does love and hate enter in this incident between Obama and Netanyahu? It must be obvious that neither of them loves the other, but do they hate each other?

Of course, Israel is closer to Iran than the US and has more to fear if Iran should obtain nuclear weapons. On the other hand, the US is not the only nation negotiating a nuclear agreement with Iran – the other nations are France, the United Kingdom, Russia, China, and Germany. Even if the US pulled out of the negotiations, the other nations could still reach an agreement without the US. However, perhaps Israel believes that an agreement without the US would be meaningless.

To add insult to injury, a few days after

Netanyahu's speech to Congress, 47 Republican senators, led by Tom Cotton, wrote a letter to Iran's leaders, undercutting President Barack Obama's efforts to negotiate a nuclear agreement with those same leaders, warning them that any agreement reached with Iran by US President Barack Obama would have to have the support of Congress in the US, without which such an agreement would solely exist between President Obama and Supreme Leader Ayatollah Khamenei. Peter Spiro, a constitutional law professor at Temple University, argued that the Republican letter is a case that "fits pretty neatly with the elements of a Logan Act violation." But he also agreed with Steve Vladeck, a constitutional law professor at American University, that there is no chance these senators would ever face prosecution.

The White House insists that an agreement with Iran does not require the approval of legislators. President Obama accused the 47 senators of interfering in his negotiations and making an "unusual coalition" with Iran's hard-line religious leaders. US Secretary of State, John Kerry, slammed the letter in a Senate hearing; he said his reaction to it had been "utter disbelief." Vice President Joe Biden also took strong exception to the letter. Even Iranian Supreme Leader Ayatollah Khamenei joined top US officials in blasting the letter, but he also lashed out at the world powers, saying: "Of course, I'm concerned because the other side [of the negotiating table, namely Britain, France, Germany, Russia, China, and the US] is into deception, trickery, and backstabbing."

If anything, John Boehner inviting the Israeli Prime Minister Benjamin Netanyahu to speak to Congress, criticizing the US President's negotiations with Iran, plus the follow-up action by 47 US Senators, makes the rest of the world lose confidence in US politicians and their political system.

In the final analysis, our love/hate relationships with each other must be carefully examined for hidden agendas and authenticity – what does Prime Minister Netanyahu mean when he assures the US Congress that he has the utmost respect for President Obama, but hopefully Congress stops Obama's negotiations with Iran? Are these assertions contradictory? Does Netanyahu want his pie and eat it too? And what are the 47 Republican senators trying to accomplish? Do they want to help, hinder, or stop President Obama's negotiations with Iran?

I have recently come to the conclusion that love is predominantly everywhere, even where hate exists, which may surprise my readers. We know, for example, that Adolf Hitler hated the Jews, and it is quite possible that he also loved to hate them. If this is so, it is easy to understand that love can be present where hate exists. People who love to eat may hate to become obese; people who love to smoke may hate to contract cancer; and so on. Examples of such love-hate relationships are countless. If you hate something or someone, just ask yourself where love comes into the equation. I am sure that you will not only find an answer but also come to the conclusion that hate is an unhealthy emotion, especially if you love to hate.

Incidents regarding love/hate relationships between our esteemed world leaders are some of the examples this book aims to explore, but before we explore the love/hate relationships of our esteemed world leaders, it may be useful to remind ourselves what true love is all about. Some of us are familiar with Biblical accounts of love, but it is the love of Jesus Christ that stands out.

It is very hard for us really to imagine what Jesus felt like when He was crucified. Try to imagine being stripped of your clothes, laid on a wooden cross, arms stretched out, hands and feet nailed to the cross with spikes, then hanging from these spikes with the cross erected, experiencing excruciating pain, bleeding profusely, and looking down at your enemies, who only laugh at, jeer, mock, and scorn you; and, with what little strength you have left, you look up and say, "Father forgive them, for they know not what they do."* If you can imagine doing this, you can also imagine what Jesus meant by "love your enemies."

You say, "Impossible; I can't do this; I can't even imagine it; it can't be done." However, this is what happened to Jesus. Jesus had told his disciples "Love your enemies."† Later, on the cross, suffering severely from the atrocities of his enemies, he actually practiced what he had preached to his disciples. The love of Jesus, at that moment, is the greatest love imaginable, and he proved it can be done; he put it into practice.

However, Jesus may have meant "Be charitable to your enemies." Compare two translations of 1 Corinthians 13:1-8: In the King James Version, Paul the Apostle talks about charity, but in Luther's version Paul talks about love. Ask yourself, which is the truer and more meaningful translation? Obviously, as I have already mentioned in my book *Thoughts in a Maze,* translations are extremely important, since wrong translations can often alter the original meaning that authors had in mind. If "love" and "charity" in these two translations are interchangeable, Jesus's command to "love your enemies" may take on an entirely different meaning!

---

* See Luke 23:34
†See Matthew 5:44

Lies That Changed History

Lies that changed history usually include deceits in the political arena, but can also include other events. One of the earliest ruses is the Trojan horse. The story goes that during the Trojan War, circa 1194 to 1184 BC, the Greeks constructed a huge wooden horse, hiding a select force of men inside, as a gift to the Trojans to enter the City of Troy, which the Trojans accepted, and, thus, with the select force of men the Greeks won the war. This story comes from Greek mythology and neither the war nor the gift of the horse may in fact have happened, but the paradox is this: even if the Trojan horse never existed, it nevertheless changed history, because its ruse in various forms was used throughout the centuries. Take the allied nations' deception of the Germans with their Operation Fortitude during World War II, which misled the German High Command as to the true location of the allied nations' planned invasion of France, when they landed *their* "Trojan horse" in Normandy rather than in Pas-de-Calais, where the Germans anticipated it.

All is fair in love and war, as the saying goes, which includes the above-cited deception, but it should exclude outright dishonorable actions. For example, Adolf Hitler agreed in writing to nonaggression pacts with Poland and Russia, and he broke both of them. Again, we have lies that changed history, but I think such dishonorable lies are despicable. I have signed many contracts during my construction career, but breaking signed, and even verbal, contracts is always a no-no. This no-no should also apply to politicians.

In 1938, British Prime Minister Neville Chamberlain had met with German Chancellor Adolf Hitler to discuss Hitler's demand for the Sudetenland. At that time, Hitler had promised Chamberlain he would have no more demands for territory in Europe, but in 1939 he invaded Czechoslovakia. When Chamberlain realized that Hitler had lied to him, he promised that if Germany were to invade Poland Britain would defend her. And with Germany's eventual invasion of Poland, World War II was underway.

However, Germany's Propaganda Ministry issued a poster with a hand and an index finger pointing at a Jew with the words: "Der ist schuld am Kriege!" (He is to blame for the war!). A lie, of course, but it tried to accomplish two things: assuage the Germans who hated another war, and rile them up against the Jews for causing this hated war, which eventually led to the biggest holocaust in history.

The twentieth century abounded with political lies that changed history. An example is the intriguing meeting of "The Big Three," US President Franklin D. Roosevelt, British Prime Minister Winston Churchill, and Russian Marshall Joseph Stalin, which is known as the Yalta Conference, held at the Livadia Palace in the Crimea from 4th to 11th of February 1945, where The Big Three agreed on the post-war configuration of Europe. Roosevelt and Churchill were suspicious of Stalin's potential communistic agenda, and requested Stalin's commitment to support the nations of Eastern Europe in their endeavor to restore their sovereign rights and self-government as well as democratic elections. Stalin promised to support them in this endeavor, having no intentions to allow it to happen. What Roosevelt and Churchill did not know was that Stalin had already reached a pact with German Chancellor Adolf Hitler to divvy up Eastern Europe between them, and although the pact had been broken by Hitler, Stalin had no inclination to let Roosevelt and Churchill talk him into abandoning his ambitions regarding the control of these nations. Besides, the Red Army had already advanced through most of Eastern Europe to defeat Germany, and, thus, was already in control of these regions.

Stalin was especially interested in Poland – all of

Poland and not just half of Poland, as he had agreed with Hitler. In a secret meeting between Stalin and Roosevelt, Roosevelt unilaterally ceded Polish territory to Stalin in order to get Stalin's support in the Pacific War. Churchill did not know about this arrangement beforehand. This did not help the tension that already existed between Roosevelt and Churchill. Eventually, Stalin's lie to accommodate Roosevelt and Churchill's proposal regarding the sovereignty of the Eastern European nations took nearly half a century to undo and caused immeasurable tragedies. Also of interest in this regard is that the Polish Prime Minister Stanislaw Mikolajcyk was deliberately left out of the Yalta Conference and not informed of its conclusions; his persistence caused Churchill annoyance, and Churchill berated him for his refusal to conform to Stalin's wishes.

Of interest in this regard is that Britain was so incensed over Hitler's attack on Poland in 1939 that it declared war on Germany, but Britain did not declare war on Russia, even though Russia attacked Poland from the east after Germany attacked Poland from the west. Ironically, at the Yalta Conference the US and Britain made it possible for Stalin to carry out what he had secretly planned with Hitler in 1939.

Nonetheless, Joseph Stalin never saw the end result of his lie at the Yalta Conference, since he died on 5 March 1953.

However, Nikita Khrushchev, First Secretary of the Communist Party of the Soviet Union from 1953 to 1964, and Soviet Premier, from 1958 to 1964, although he was responsible for the **de-Stalinization** of the Soviet Union, he had no qualms carrying on with Stalin's tradition of lies. When the Soviet Union supplied Cuba with weapons, the US was mightily concerned about this, but Khrushchev assured the US several times that these were defensive and not offensive weapons. However, in the morning of 16 October 1962, US President John F. Kennedy got a rude awakening by his National Security Adviser, McGeorge Bundy, with photographic evidence of Khrushchev's lie. What followed in the next thirteen days was an escalation to start a potential nuclear war by the US against the Soviet Union, which was in the end averted only because reason prevailed. Kennedy and Khrushchev reached an agreement that satisfied both. How much can one write about a lie that nearly caused a nuclear world war? Easily an entire book, but enough of these have already been written. Suffice it to say that the danger of a nuclear world war in the twentieth century was very real and dependent on two individuals who were ready to carry it out.

Another lie in the 1960s, although without the danger of causing a nuclear war, has resulted in the loss of many lives. Prompted by a North Vietnamese attack, which never occurred, on a US destroyer in the Gulf of Tonkin, namely the USS Maddox, on 4 August 1966, the US air attacked North Vietnamese targets, and, in that way, became fully engaged in the Vietnamese War.

The US Vietnamese involvement started with Operational Plan 34A, which was a highly classified US program of covert actions against the Democratic Republic of Vietnam (North Vietnam) consisting of agent team insertions, aerial reconnaissance missions, and naval sabotage operations. Though begun in 1961 by the Central Intelligence Agency, in 1964 the program was transferred to the Military Assistance Command, Vietnam Studies and Observations Group (SOG) during Operation Parasol/Switchback. The SOG was the cover name for a multi-service unconventional warfare task force under the direct guidance and control of the Pentagon.[*]

On the night of 30-31 July 1964, the USS Maddox was on station in the Gulf of Tonkin when an OPLAN 34A raid was launched by the South Vietnamese against the North Vietnamese Hon Me Island. After observing North Vietnamese patrol torpedo boats pursuing the South Vietnamese vessels that had attacked Hon Me, the Maddox withdrew from

---

the area and later denied she had been aware of the attack on Hon Me. That pretended ignorance set the stage for a showdown between North Vietnamese forces and the US Navy. On 2 August 1964 at 1440, the Maddox detected three North Vietnamese patrol boats approaching her. Captain John Herrick ordered his gun crews to open fire if the fast-approaching trio closed to within 10,000 yards of the destroyer, and at 1505 three 5-inch shots were fired across the bow of the closest boat. In return, the lead vessel launched a torpedo, and the second boat launched two torpedoes but was hit by the destroyer's gun fire. Re-engaging, the first boat launched another torpedo and some gun fire, but the Maddox's shell fire heavily damaged the vessel. Flying overhead, Navy Commander James Stockdale passed over the unscathed Maddox at 1530, minutes after the 22-minute surface engagement had ended. The US pilots made multiple firing runs on the enemy vessels. The two lead boats were heavily damaged, and the third was left dead and burning in the water. The next day, the Maddox resumed her Desoto patrol, and President Lyndon B. Johnson ordered the USS Turner Joy to join the Maddox on patrol off the North Vietnamese coast. That night, the South Vietnamese staged more OPLAN 34A raids.[*]

---

[*] Naval History Magazine – February 2008, Volume 22, Number 1, by Lieutenant Commander Pat Paterson, US Navy.

At this point, North Vietnamese installations had been attacked four separate times in five days.

On the morning of 4 August, contrasting clear conditions two days earlier, thunderstorms reduced visibility and increased wave heights to six feet. In addition, the Maddox's long-range air-search radar and the Turner Joy's fire-control radar were inoperative. Nevertheless, at 2040, the Maddox reported she was tracking unidentified vessels. However, targets would disappear and reappear, and the two US destroyers maneuvered to evade perceived enemy boat attacks, and reported automatic-weapons fire, torpedo attacks, sightings of torpedo waves, and numerous radar and surface contacts. By the time they broke off their counterattacks, they had fired 249 five-inch shells, 123 three-inch shells, and four or five depth charges. Navy Commander James Stockdale made runs at low altitude parallel to the US destroyers' course looking for enemy vessels and later reported, "I had the best seat in the house to watch that event, and our destroyers were just shooting at phantom targets – there were no PT boats there…there was nothing there but black water and American firepower." Captain John J. Herrick also began to have his doubts and declared, "Review of action makes many reported contacts and torpedoes fired appear doubtful. Freak weather effects on radar, and overeager sonar men may have accounted for many reports. No actual visual sightings by Maddox. Suggest complete evaluation before any further action is taken." However, a little over an hour later, Captain Herrick sent another report in which he changed his previous story: "Certain that original ambush was bona fide. Details of action following present a confusing picture. Have interviewed witnesses who made positive visual sightings of cockpit lights or similar passing near Maddox. Several reported torpedoes were probably boats themselves which were observed to make several close passes on Maddox. Own ship screw noises on rudders may have accounted for some. At present, cannot even estimate number of boats involved. Turner Joy reports two torpedoes passed near her." Unlike Captain Herrick, Navy Commander James Stockdale had no doubt about what had happened: "We were about to launch a war under false pretenses, in the face of the on-scene military commander's advice to the contrary."

Obviously, in view of these conflicting reports, US President Lyndon B. Johnson should have ordered a more thorough investigation before ordering an air attack on North Vietnam.

There never was a second attack on US ships in the Tonkin Gulf in early August 1964, and subsequently declassified documents provide evidence that suggests a disturbing and deliberate attempt by US Secretary of Defense Robert McNamara to distort the evidence and mislead Congress and the public.[*]

If you think that the phantom attacks on 4 August 1964 were a poor excuse for the US to start a war with North Vietnam, compare it to the Gleiwitz incident, where Nazi forces posing as Poles attacked the German radio station Sender Gleiwitz in Upper Silesia on 31 August 1939. The goal was to use the staged attack as a pretext for invading Poland on 1 September 1939. Similar German-Polish border incidents had also been staged by the Nazis, to give the appearance of Polish aggression against Germany. On the same day, in a speech in the Reichstag, German Chancellor Adolf Hitler cited the border incidents, with three of them called very serious, as justification for Germany's invasion of Poland. Just a few days earlier, on 22 August, he had told his generals, "I will provide a propagandistic casus belli. Its credibility doesn't matter. The victor will not be asked whether he told the truth."[†]

Obviously, leaders who want a war will use any means and excuse to justify it. Nevertheless, people who think the Gleiwitz Incident was the cause of

[*] Naval History Magazine – February 2008, Volume 22, Number 1, by Lieutenant Commander Pat Paterson, US Navy.
[†] Source: Wikipedia under *The Gleiwitz Incident*.

World War II are wrong, as the secret pact between Stalin and Hitler earlier in August 1939 proves.

Lies abound the bombing of Dresden two-and-a-half months prior to the end of World War II in Europe. 722 heavy bombers of the British Royal Air Force and 527 of the United States Army Air Force dropped more than 3,900 tons of high-explosive bombs and incendiary devices on the city, resulting in a firestorm that destroyed 1,600 acres of the city center.[*] The following comments are neither true nor false: Some say that the Allies, expecting a near end of the war, wanted to get rid of their surplus of bombs; some say the Western Allies wanted to impress the Russians. Others defend the bombings because of the existence of factories to support the German war effort. However, these factories were not located in the city center. Some say that neither the factories outside the city nor the communication infrastructure, such as bridges, were targeted by the bombers. The estimate of civilians killed by the bombing varies from 25,000 to 500,000 depending on the historian reporting it. This great variance is probably due to the number of refugees that had come to the city.

Here is what Winston Churchill had to say about the bombing of Dresden, in a memo dated 28 March 1945 sent by telegram to General Ismay for the British

---

[*] Source: Wikipedia under *The Destruction of Dresden*.

Chiefs of Staff and the Chief of the Air Staff, he wrote:

> It seems to me that the moment has come when the question of bombing of German cities simply for the sake of increasing the terror, though under other pretexts, should be reviewed. Otherwise we shall come into control of an utterly ruined land… The destruction of Dresden remains a serious query against the conduct of Allied bombing. I am of the opinion that military objectives must henceforward be more strictly studied in our own interests than that of the enemy. The Foreign Secretary has spoken to me on this subject, and I feel the need for more precise concentration upon military objectives such as oil and communications behind the immediate battle-zone, rather than on mere acts of terror and wanton destruction, however impressive.[*]

These examples suffice to give us warning, although many books could be written about them.

---

[*] Source: Wikipedia under *The Destruction of Dresden*.

Prejudicial Movies

Some movies are designed to create prejudice. For example, a movie may exaggerate criminal behaviors, or racial, religious, and sexual differences, which are specifically designed to amplify an existing prejudice. I think one such movie is *Judgment at Nuremberg.*

In this movie, a Tribunal of three American judges sits to render its judgment regarding alleged crimes against humanity of four German judges and prosecutors. The movie is a fictionalized version of an actual tribunal that was held in 1947.

I am assuming that the screenwriter, Abby Mann, and the producer/director, Stanley Kramer, probably wanted to make the point that American justice outshines the justice doled out by the judges of the Third Reich. If this assumption is correct, the movie should have adhered more closely to the American accepted rules of evidence. For example, the tribunal should have disallowed Rudolph Peterson, Maria Wallner, and Elsa Lindnow to testify, because their testimony is not the best evidence. The best evidence consists of the transcripts of the original trials that governed the German judges. The tribunal allowing the testimony by these three people can only serve to distort or prejudice the evidence recorded at the original trials. American appellate courts usually do not allow witnesses to re-testify at their sessions; they rely on the transcripts of the original trials.

Herr Oscar Rolfe, the defense attorney representing the accused German judge Ernst Janning, instead of moving to strike the testimony of these witnesses, proceeded to cross-examine them. During his cross-examination of these witnesses, Oscar Rolfe sounded a lot like a mean prosecutor of the Third Reich. If he intended to do damage to his defense of Ernst Janning, he succeeded, or, rather, the screenwriter and the director of the movie succeeded. It was a very prejudicial part of the movie. In particular, Oscar Rolfe's harassing cross-examination of Maria Wallner, trying to get her to admit that she'd had a sexual relationship with Lehman Feldenstein (at the time of his arrest, Lehman Feldenstein was old enough to be her grandfather), caused Maria extreme stress, and Ernst Janning stood up and said, "Are you going to do this again?" (He probably meant, "Are *we* going to do this again?" because Oscar Rolfe was not involved in the original trial of Lehman Feldenstein.) This question prompted Colonel Tad Parker,[*] the head

---

[*] Colonel Parker was extremely biased against the Germans. In a bar in Grand Hotel, Colonel Parker, drunk, appears at a table where

of the prosecution team, to address the court, "Your Honor. I believe the defendant wishes to make a statement," and upon Judge Haywood's question, Ernst Janning confirmed this.

The next day, Ernst Janning made his statement. He began by saying that the Feldenstein case was the most significant trial of the period, and to understand it you must understand the period in which it happened: there was "a fever of disgrace, of indignity, of hunger…fear of today, fear of tomorrow, fear of our neighbors, fear of ourselves. Only when you understand that can you understand what Hitler meant to us…he said to us, 'Lift up your heads! Be proud to be German! There are devils among us. Communists, Liberals, Jews, Gypsies! Once the devils will be destroyed, your miseries will be destroyed!'" Ernst Janning continues with their early justification of agreeing with Hitler – for their love of the country. He goes on by saying, "I had reached my verdict on the

---

Judges Haywood and Ives are sitting, and voices his disgust with the German defence attorney's cross-examination of Rudolph Peterson. Judge Ives tells him, "The trouble with you, Colonel, is that you'd like to indict the whole country. That might be emotionally satisfying for you, but it's not exactly practical – and hardly fair." After a pause, Colonel Parker replies, "There are no Nazis in Germany. Didn't you know that, Judge? The Eskimos invaded Germany and took over. That's how all those terrible things happened. It wasn't the fault of the Germans. It was those damn Eskimos!" Colonel Parker leaves, and Judge Ives said to Judge Haywood, "You know, that's one problem with the prosecution. It's filled with radicals like Parker."

Feldenstein case before I ever came into the courtroom. I would have found him guilty whatever the evidence. It was not a trial at all. It was a sacrificial ritual in which Feldenstein, the Jew, was the helpless victim…" Oscar Rolfe interjects: "Your Honor, I must interrupt. The defendant is not aware of what he is saying…" Ernst Janning cries out, "I am aware! I am aware! My defense counsel would have you believe that we were not aware of concentration camps! Not aware? Where were we?! Where were we when Hitler began shrieking his hatred in the Reichstag? Where were we when our neighbors were being dragged out of their houses in the middle of the night to Dachau…Were we deaf, dumb, and blind?!...Maybe we didn't know the details. But if we didn't know, it was because we didn't want to know." Emil Hahn, another of the defendants, cries out, "Traitor! Traitor!" Ernst Janning then ends his statement by pointing out some of the shortcomings of his co-defendants.

Ernst Janning's statement neatly fits this prejudicial movie. His description how the German people fell under Hitler's spell certainly did not apply to many Germans and his assertion that "…if we didn't know, it was because we didn't want to know," is not only untrue but illogical. Most Germans did *not* know about the atrocities that occurred in concentration camps. How, then, could they not want to know what they did not know? However, Emil Hahn's outcry: "Traitor! Traitor!" gives Ernst Janning's nonsensical assertion credence. Finally, Ernst Janning ends his statement by telling the court the so-called "truth" about his fellow defendants, but this is nothing more than an opinion, which should have been struck under judicial rules, but since it was designed to endorse the overall prejudice of the movie, nobody objected to it.

Furthermore, the tribunal should have disallowed the concentration-camp film evidence submitted by Colonel Parker without laying a foundation that proved the German judges had prior knowledge of what was going to happen to people whom they convicted and sent to concentration camps. American judges, too, are not held responsible for people they send to prison and who happen to get killed there. The American rules of evidence call for laying a foundation before evidence is admitted.

Some critics insist that the tribunals in Nuremberg after World War II were nothing more than kangaroo courts.* There may be some truth to this

---

* Wikipedia: A kangaroo court is a judicial tribunal or assembly that blatantly disregards recognized standards of law or justice, and often carries little or no official standing in the territory within which it resides. Merriam Webster defines it as a "mock court in which the principles of law and justice are disregarded or <u>perverted</u>." The term

insistence, especially when it comes to accused leaders like Hermann Goering, who was probably judged guilty before the tribunal hearings began. Any criminal court that is held without a jury must be suspect as a kangaroo court. Even Abby Mann, in his Author's Introduction to his 2001 publication of the screenplay for *Judgment at Nuremberg*, pointed out the pitfalls of a military tribunal:

> The procedures of a military tribunal are: Military officers, who are dependent on their superiors for promotion, would act as judge and jury. A two-thirds vote of commission members would be sufficient to convict and impose any sentence. The defendant could be barred from seeing the evidence against him. The defendant could not appeal. The trials could be held in secret.
>
> As Anthony Lewis said in a [sic] article in *The New York Times*, "What confidence could the world have in the justice of such a proceeding? Such confidence is crucial. The Nuremberg trials of Nazi leaders, in open court before an

---

may also apply to a court held by a legitimate judicial authority who intentionally disregards the court's legal or ethical obligations. A kangaroo court is often held to give the appearance of a fair and just trial, even though the verdict has in reality already been decided before the trial has begun.

international tribunal, had a profound effect in bringing Germans back to democracy and humanity." [Obviously, Anthony Lewis did not consider the Nuremberg tribunals kangaroo courts.]

In any case, when a movie is deliberately designed to disregard accepted evidence procedures it makes one wonder to what extent is was aimed to create prejudice.

There cannot be any doubt that crimes against humanity were committed in Germany by some of the Nazis during the Third Reich. The question is: Who were the Nazis responsible for these crimes? Leni Riefenstahl even doubted that Hitler knew all that was going on.

I was born in 1934, one year after Hitler rose to power, and I was eleven years old when World War II ended. What did I know of concentration camps – KZ (pronounced: Kaah-tset) Lager, as they were known in Germany? Well, I knew they existed, and I knew that some of my mother's friends were arrested and sent to these camps, because they had revolted against the Nazis (and they were not Jews, by the way) but neither I nor any of my acquaintances knew what happened to most of the people who were sent to these camps. We did not hear from them again – that's all we knew. I have no doubt that even German judges did not know any more than ordinary people did, as incredible as that may sound. I can even believe Leni Riefenstahl's doubt that Hitler knew everything that was going on. In fact, Hermann Goering, Hitler's second in command, insisted at the first tribunal sessions in Nuremberg that he had no idea about what was going on in the concentration camps and condemned the actions, and since he was quite honest about everything else he said, his denial of knowledge of the KZ Lager atrocities is credible, in my opinion.

Chief Judge Dan Haywood, in the movie *Judgment at Nuremberg*, made an effort to find out to what extent German people knew of the atrocities of the concentration camps. He questioned Frau Halbestadt, and he listened to Frau Bertholt's denials, but neither of them could completely convince him how little Germans knew of what was going on. What the chief judge was indirectly asking these women was if they were aware of the criminal actions[*] that were

---

[*] Such criminal actions were carried out by criminal minds and were even illegal under German law. Hundreds if not thousands of books have been written analysing the criminal mind. Most of these books analyse the ordinary criminal mind, but very few of these books analyse the type of criminal mind that was responsible for the atrocities of the Nazi-German concentration camps. What kind of mind takes pleasure in turning on the poison-gas tap to kill hundreds and hundreds of thousands of innocent people? Surely such a mind cannot be considered normal even by the most understanding of analysts. And if such a mind is abnormal, what makes it abnormal? Is

being carried out in these German concentration camps. His question is akin to asking ordinary people in the streets of America to what extent they are aware of criminal actions being carried out in their jails (these criminal actions could include prisoner rapes, drug trafficking, and even murder). Most Americans would probably answer that they are not aware of any criminal actions being carried out in their jails.

However, even if Chief Judge Dan Haywood could believe that ordinary Germans did not know much, he had problems believing that the German judges he was charged to render judgment on were equally innocent. I do not have the same problems. I knew people who were Nazis just to maintain a decent job. I'm sure that none of them knew what was happening in these concentration camps. I still remember the outraged horror of most Germans after the war, when they found out about the concentration camp atrocities. Nevertheless, I can understand Judge Haywood's disbelief, coming from America, where the media turn over every stone to find fault. This did not happen in Germany, where the media were controlled by the Nazis.

One problem is that Germany was involved in

---

it some special sickness? Is this sickness treatable and curable? And how is such a sickness contracted in the first place? Is it inherited, part of a gene, or is it transmitted by some kind of germ or virus? Even such questions boggle the normal mind!

nine wars before World War I, starting with the Franco-Prussian War (1870-1871). These wars were mostly victorious. German soldiers had gained a reputation of being fierce fighters. This reputation helped to establish a prejudice against Germans, which made German people's claims of ignorance regarding concentration-camp atrocities less credible after World War II. It does not take much of a belief to support such an established prejudice. If I like someone, and trust him, I'm inclined to believe him, but if I'm guided by a prejudice against him, I'm inclined to disbelieve him even if he tells the truth!

Prejudicial movies are sometimes accidentally created: Abby Mann may not have deliberately designed his script to create prejudice, but it exists nevertheless. I have an observation: if the screenwriter and the producer/director are of one mind, inclusions of prejudices in the movie are more likely; otherwise, the producer/director would ensure the exclusions of prejudices.

I offer for your consideration and contemplation the last two paragraphs of Abby Mann's Author's Introduction to his 2001 publication of the screenplay:

The words ring in my ears that Robert Kempner had told me years ago when I asked him whether the Nuremberg trials were necessary. His answer:

"Without them all these people [who died in the concentration camps] would have died for no reason and no one was responsible and it will happen again." The issues that we dealt with in *Judgment at Nuremberg* unfortunately are still with us. [In this last comment, Abby Mann referred to Slobodan Milosovich who was charged in 2001 by an international court with the murder of thousands of Kosovo Albanians; he also referred to some critics trying to justify the destruction of the twin towers of the World Trade Center complex, and the deaths of thousands of innocent people, by blaming the United States for taking sides in the Israeli-Palestinian conflict.]

In part, it was McCarthyism in the U.S.A. that convinced Abby Mann to proceed with *Judgment at Nuremberg*. While McCarthyists did not use gas chambers, "people were being destroyed financially and jailed because of their political beliefs and even because of whom they knew," wrote Abby Mann. "The question was on the table: Could what happened in Germany happen elsewhere?" he asked, and with this question in mind, he proceeded with the script for *Judgment at Nuremberg*.

Abby Mann, being of Jewish ancestry himself, did not have an easy task putting his own bias aside.

One must remember that the Jewish people always loved the German people. Before Nazi rule, Germany had been a very fertile country for the Jewish intellect, making it hard to understand how the German people could have tolerated the blatant anti-Semitism by the Nazis, which eventually led to genocide. The broken relationship between the Jewish people and the German people that has been created by an irresponsible horde of Nazi criminals may take many years, if not centuries, to rebuild!

Some of Life's Sadnesses

Brexit is surely one of life's political sadnesses. It proves again that voters who do not understand the consequences of their decisions should not be asked to vote on the issue. A small example of such a dilemma occurred in my home city when Edmonton voters were asked to decide whether or not to get rid of their municipal airport. Most voters never used this municipal airport, did not care one way or another, and did not understand the consequences of their decision to those who did use the airport – a true sadness!

Russian President Vladimir Putin says 'Brexit' is the choice made by the British nation and is a comprehensible one, as "no one wants to feed weak economies." Russia has not and does not plan to interfere with the results of the referendum, he added. "I think it's comprehensible why this happened: first, no one wants to feed and subsidize poorer economies, to support other states, support entire nations," the Russian president said at the Shanghai Cooperation Organization summit in Tashkent. "Apparently the British people are not satisfied with the way problems are being solved in the security sphere, these problems have become more acute lately with the migration processes," Putin said, suggesting the second reason for the British people to have voted 'out.' The Russian president's comments come in reply to UK Prime Minister David Cameron's claims that "Putin would be happy if the UK left the EU."[*]

Despite Putin's denial of Cameron's comment, Putin is smart enough to realize that a divided Europe is easier for Russia to deal with than a united Europe – divide and conquer, as was demonstrated by one of Aesop's fables. Here is a paraphrased version:

A father had sons who were constantly quarreling with each other. One day he called them together, showed them a bundle of sticks, and asked each of them to break the bundle. Each tried with all his strength but couldn't do it. Then, the father unbundled the sticks and easily broke them. The sons thought this was unfair. He then addressed them and said: "My sons, if you are of one mind, and unite to assist each other, you will be as this fagot, uninjured by all attempts of your enemies; but if you are divided among yourselves, you will be broken as easily as these sticks."

[*] Source: https://www.google.ca/amp/s/www.rt.com/document/576d2b13c4618818628b4570/amp#

Continuing with life's sadnesses, I like Sandra Pawula's comments on sadness. Here is an excerpt from her write-up *Why Sadness is the Key to True Happiness*:

> Sadness comes when things change – a relationship ends, someone dies, we're fired from a job, illness descends, a friend is physically hurt, a disaster happens. Sadness introduces us to impermanence and can help us learn to let go. Change is the only constant in life. Until we learn to accept change gracefully, we'll always suffer. There's a blessing in embracing the beauty of impermanence. Through doing so, we will come to value every precious moment of this life and live in a far saner and more fulfilling way.

However, in this chapter I am limiting my comments to sadnesses that could be avoided with some determination and comment on some ordinary situations with a sad aspect that we most often encounter in life. Some of these situations are seemingly absurd, incongruous, or even contradictory, yet, in fact, may be quite factual. Let me give you an example of such an incongruous situation: I know a man whom I dislike because he has betrayed my trust;

yet, my strong belief in Jesus Christ's philosophy to "love thy enemy" demands me to love this rascal. This seemingly incongruous situation takes place often enough between parents and children. The sadness in this example is not the loss of trust I had incurred but the cause of that loss of trust. Presumably, I could rebuild my trust in this man over time, but I could probably not change upcoming causes of loss of trust, just as one cannot change the spots of a leopard or the stripes of a zebra. In other words, beware if you are dealing with a blackguard.

Nevertheless, even the loss of trust is a serious situation and always sad. For instance, a spy depends on trust to do his or her job. In fact, a double agent depends on trust by both organizations, and/or countries: the one he or she is spying for, and the one against whom he or she is spying, and when a spy organization suspects the existence of a double agent among its members, trust is usually lost between all members. In ordinary life, we need much trust to get along. We trust our doctors; we trust our lawyers; we trust our bankers; we trust our accountants; we trust our spouses; and we trust our friends, unless and until our trusts have been betrayed, as in the example given above. But in this example, I only assumed that the man might be my friend. When I'm an offender, a friend will point this out to me, and if the assumed friend points my offence out to others, he is really not a friend; so, my loss is only the trust I'd had in him, not his friendship. In any case, a loss of trust always results in sadness.

By and large, most of life's sadnesses are not that complicated. Take a couple's divorce: it is definitely one of life's sadnesses, but sometimes couples recognize their mistake of creating this sadness and get back together – sadness resolved! However, not all sadnesses can be this simply resolved. For example, it is a sadness when we become dependent on daily work for mere survival, perhaps work we do not even like, and this situation is not easily resolved. It is also sad when we have to lie to be nice, and when we even teach our children to lie to be nice. At the same time, we teach our children that honesty is the best policy. I'm sure our children must wonder how these two messages are compatible. This sadness is also not easily resolved, unless we want our children to become offensive.

Our increasing overdependence on technology is certainly becoming more and more sad. The more we depend on technology, the more we dislike and avoid menial tasks. We are told by our technological experts that eventually all menial tasks will be performed by robots. We are not there yet, but we are moving rapidly in that direction. But consider it sad when we become so dependent on technology that we disrespect the value of menial tasks that must still be performed.

In the late 1960s and early 1970s, we were actively getting into computers, and we were glad that this would eventually lead to the elimination of paper. Almost a half century later, this has not yet happened. In fact, it seems like we are using as much if not more paper than before the event of computers – all at the expense of our forests. And the loss of our forests adds to global warming, which decreases the Arctic and Antarctic ice. This in turn increases the water levels of our oceans, which causes a loss of land mass and possibly the loss of structures affected by the loss of land mass. In addition, the increased use of cars and industries that are powered by fossil fuels also increases global warming, and this sad domino effect of global warming is irreversible. However, global warming could be slowed down, if not stopped, by determined and resolute actions of our governments. Governments' inaction to slow down global warming is certainly one of our lives' sadnesses. People who use bicycles instead of fossil-fuel-powered cars are certainly trying to slow down global warming, so why not governments?

Our available foods, whether manufactured or right from farms and orchards, create all kinds of sad conditions to harm us. Because of the various pesticides being used by farms and orchards against pests, or the refinements and preservatives being used in manufacturing our foods, we no longer feel comfortable unless our foods are guaranteed to be organic. Refined foods seem to be especially harmful to our health. Also some fast foods, although tasty, can be harmful to our health, especially when they give us little nutritional value, and when we are substituting good taste at the expense of good nutrition, then obesity, diabetes and other sickness is on the rise.

Another of life's sadnesses is our obsession with possessions. I have recently started to get rid of my possessions, especially those possessions that I have foolishly acquired when I was young and seldom, if ever, used. People are too captivated with ownership. In truth, we do not own anything; we just use them for a while.

One of people's greatest assets is the human mind. Regrettably, many people do not use their minds to their own or to society's advantage. Take superstition: It is often substituted for common sense, and, unfortunately, people who substitute superstition for common sense actually believe that it makes a lot of sense.

Fortunately, in modern times irrational beliefs are on the decrease, but they still exist in surprising numbers, which is sad. Irrational beliefs include beliefs that women and certain races are inferior. From this standpoint, all kinds of atrocities are instigated. It is hard to believe, for example, how women are still treated in most countries, especially in the Arab world. The belief that women are inferior to men is a chauvinistic and arrogant attitude; it is based on men's physical power rather than their mental power, which is no more compelling than that of women. But men who beat their wives defy logic – any logic: Western logic as well as Eastern logic. Disrespecting people, especially women, and their human rights is a very sad state of affairs.

The contemporary harsh treatment of women in the Arab regions south and east of the Mediterranean Sea is in stark contrast with the ancient treatment of women in the northern regions of the Mediterranean Sea, such as Italy and Greece, where women were venerated to the point of making goddesses out of them. To wit: Aphrodite, Artemis, Athena, Demeter, Hera, Hestia, Maia, and so on.

I have heard it said, but I do not remember by whom, that every human being has at least one book in him or her, which is probably his or her history, experience, and philosophy, and it would be sad if this book is never written or if it is lost. Parents usually pass their wisdom on to their children verbally, but a written record of their history, experiences, and philosophy would also be much appreciated by their children and children's children. I know in my case I have had only a few bits of information when it comes to my parents' history, experiences, and beliefs. I tried to capture these bits of information in some of my books, but a written account of them by my parents would have been extremely helpful. This is one of the reasons why I wrote most of my books with my history, experiences, and beliefs, and hopefully my daughters and grandchildren will get some useful information from them. Had I not written these books, it would indeed be one of life's sadnesses, and the same applies to every other human being. I believe that all human beings owe it to other human beings to pass on the lessons they have learned in their lives. This is a tremendous benefit to our human evolution.

The conception that eventually we must give back all that we have acquired in our lifetime is not new, it comes from Ecclesiastes 5:15: "As he came from his mother's womb he shall go again, naked as he came, and shall take nothing for his toil that he may carry away in his hand." This is something greedy people fail to grasp.

Greedy people take all they can get and give very little back. This applies to some nations as well, namely those that seek to increase their territory at the expense of other nations – another of life's sadnesses.

One last comment: when a person loses his or her mind due to dementia or Alzheimer's disease, it is as sad for the victim as it is for the victim's loved ones. You would expect that our scientists should have found a cure for these conditions by now, but no! It seems that it is easier for them to fly a man to our moon or to the planet Mars. The failure of our scientists to find a cure for dementia and Alzheimer's disease is truly one more of life's sadnesses.

Dubious Leadership

A leader has to be loving, fair, tolerant, well balanced, not leaning too far right nor too far left, charismatic, and aiming to achieve the maximum good for the maximum number of people. Let us examine how our world leaders measure up to these criteria.

Going back to the early twentieth century, Germany already experienced dubious leadership by Kaiser Wilhelm II. He started his reign in 1888, at age twenty-nine, and soon had disagreements with Otto von Bismarck, Germany's first Chancellor. While some of Bismarck's actions would also qualify under dubious leadership, his diplomatic foreign policy kept Europe at peace from 1871 to 1890. Kaiser Wilhelm II dismissed him in 1890, although in a letter dated 18 March 1890 Bismarck requested his dismissal. He had been in office from 23 November 1862, when King Wilhelm I had appointed him as Minister President of Prussia, and in 1871 Bismarck formed the German Empire, also known as the Second Reich. After Bismarck's dismissal, the Russians expected a reversal of policy in Berlin and acted quickly to come to terms with France.

As expected by the Russians and with Bismarck out of the way, Kaiser Wilhelm II was free to pursue his contentious policy, plotting with senior generals in favor of war of aggression. They decided to support Austria-Hungary in case it were forced into a war, which they expected and which occurred in 1914, after a Yugoslav nationalist assassinated Archduke Franz Ferdinand, heir presumptive to the Austro-Hungarian throne. Thus, Kaiser Wilhelm II's policy was at least in part responsible for World War I.

A few years later, after Adolf Hitler formed the Third Reich from 1933 to 1945, Hitler's actions come certainly under the heading of dubious leadership. One example is his pact with Joseph Stalin in August 1939. It was supposedly a nonaggression pact, but, in reality, it was designed to divide Eastern Europe between Russia and Germany. However, this part stayed secret until after World War II. In any case, Hitler did not honor the Pact and eventually attacked Russia, which turned into a disaster for Germany. This example stresses once again that leadership requires trust, and trust requires honesty, and honesty requires truthfulness, which Hitler and Stalin lacked.

Dubious leadership was also familiar to American presidents. Former US President John F. Kennedy qualifies for this chapter with his approval on 4 April 1961 of the final invasion plan of Cuba at the Bay of Pigs, where, on 17 April 1961, 1400 Cuban exiles launched the botched invasion. This angered Cuban Prime Minister Fidel Castro, who also qualifies for this chapter, to make a deal with the Soviet Union's Premier Nikita Khrushchev to install nuclear missiles on Cuba, which also qualifies Khrushchev for this chapter. The Cuban installation of nuclear missiles by the Soviet Union eventually led to the Cuban Missile Crisis that could easily have escalated to a nuclear world war.

Former US President Lyndon B. Johnson qualifies for this chapter by his premature attack on North Vietnam as a result of faulty reports of North Vietnam's attack on US ships.

Former US President Richard Nixon qualifies because of his attempted cover-up of the Watergate scandal.

Former US President Jimmy Carter qualifies because of his failure to resolve the Iran Hostage Crisis expeditiously.

Former US President George H.W. Bush qualifies because of his failure to finish the Gulf War properly, and his son, former US President George W. Bush qualifies because of his premature attack on Iraq (to finish his father's job) rather than waiting for a United Nations' resolution for authority, which would have included all UN members.

US President Barack Obama qualifies because of his involvement in the Libya debacle, and because of his inability to resolve the ISIS crisis more expeditiously.

Former British Prime Minister Tony Blair also qualifies for this chapter because of his premature attack on Iraq instead of waiting for a United Nations' resolution for authority, which would have included all UN members.

Former British Prime Minister David Cameron qualifies because he should have used more of his influence to prevent a referendum on Brexit. It is never a good idea to take a complex issue to the people for a decision when the people do not fully comprehend the consequences and are swayed by emotions.

Israeli Prime Minister Benjamin Netanyahu qualifies because of his arrangement to speak to the US Congress on 3 March 2015 to derail US President Obama's negotiations with Iran – negotiations that intended to prevent Iran from acquiring a nuclear weapon; Netanyahu arranged this speech without the support and engagement of the Obama administration.

Russian Federation President Vladimir Putin should restrain his involvement in Ukrainian affairs.

I gave German Chancellor Angela Merkel a tribute in my book *Conclusions Volume II*, and I nominated her for membership in The Group of Twenty-Two (twenty-two of the wisest people in the world) in my book *Human Traits & Follies.* Nevertheless, I am now obliged to include her in this chapter mainly because of her immigration policy. To allow a million immigrants into Germany on short notice is certainly a doubtful policy, because it also invites the influx of potential terrorists. I began to have some doubts about Angela Merkel when she publicly supported the President of France Nicolas Sarkozy in his reelection campaign. This move may have made up the minds of the undecided voters to vote against Sarkozy, since these voters may have been suspicious of German support for him. Angela Merkel has had an excellent relationship with Nicolas Sarkozy, which was good for German-French rapport, but she may have been wiser to pay more attention to the British leadership. Furthermore, my friend Jim Lampard criticizes Angela Merkel for her stance on the eurozone (for further details of Jim's objections, see the Chapter, *The Group of Twenty-Two*).

American and European bankers qualify to be included in this chapter because even their shamefully high salaries and their bonuses gave their banks no assurance that the extremely risky loans they granted will be repaid. Furthermore, when governments had to bail them out because of defaulting loans, these bankers continued to receive their shameful salaries and bonuses, which were paid out of the bail-out monies.

I have only chosen some well-known leaders to be included in this chapter. I'm sure there are many more I could have included. Dubious leadership is rampant in the world, as the above examples and many bankruptcies will confirm.

Tsipras the Oddball

The Greek Prime Minister Alexis Tsipras seems to have a profound love for the underdog and for the Greek people. I got to know him better during my trip to Germany in late June and early July 2015. He conducted the negotiations for a Greek bailout with most of the political and financial heavies of Europe. Angela Merkel tried to inform him of the political and financial realities he was facing, but he just smiled at her. After all, he had gained his political position not by being cautious, but by throwing caution to the wind, and his own people cheered for him. Still, Tsipras secretly admired Merkel and paid close attention to her advice.

The negotiations went nowhere during June, and on 27 June 2015, Tsipras announced a referendum to decide whether or not the Greek people want to accept the joint bailout conditions proposed by the European financial heavies. He recommended a "no" vote, and the voters accommodated him, despite warnings that a "no" vote could result in Greece leaving the eurozone.

After the shock of the "no" vote subsided, Tsipras continued his negotiations with the lenders, and on 13 July came to an agreement with them to lend Greece 86 billion euros. In return, Greece agreed to increase its value-added-tax, reform its pension system, cut public spending, revoke most of Tsipras' laws except the one regarding humanitarian crisis, assuring the independence of the Hellenic Statistical Authority, recapitalize the banks, and privatize fifty billion of public assets. On 14 August, the Greek parliament backed the deal.

Then, on 20 August, Tsipras resigned the position of Prime Minister of Greece because of a rebellion of MPs from his own party and called for another election.

What puzzled me is the logic of the Greeks: the Greeks were saying forgive us our debt, and give us more money to squander, without stringent conditions attached for repayment. It reminded me of the Berliner saying "boldness wins." However, a word of caution is in order. It has been my experience that intelligent people who act illogically may have good reason for doing so; further investigation is usually warranted.

Apparently, the first bailout was not for the Greek people at all but for the banks that had granted bad loans, and the Greek people would have to repay the bailout through austerity programs. If this is true, it starts making sense that the Greek people want the creditors to cancel the debt, since the creditors or their banks ended up with most of the bailout money. Also, if a member nation is in trouble, it makes sense for other member nations to come to its aid.

The next puzzle came when Tsipras, eight days after the "no" vote, agreed to the conditions his people said "no" to. Is this logical? It makes us wonder just how serious he was in these negotiations.

A few weeks earlier, Tsipras agreed with Russia to build a gas pipeline through Greece with Russian financing – despite Washington's warning against it. When the deal was signed, Tsipras declared, "Russia is one of the most important partners for us." So, the US, the EU, and NATO must find a more attractive way to negotiate with Tsipras if they want to prevent him turning to Russia and China for help.

Greece wasn't always down. Up until 2007, Greece still produced over four percent growth per annum. Take note that Greece has the largest merchant marine in the world, exporting cement, re-bars, pharmaceuticals, beverages, agricultural products, and shipbuilding. Besides, Greece attracts a lot of tourists who spend money. Creditors should heed these facts.

Tsipras entered the public eye of Greek politics in 2006 when he ran for mayor of Athens and came in third, but he won a seat on the Municipality of Athens council. He refused to run for the Greek parliament in 2007, opting to complete his term on the municipal council of Athens. However, he also served as leader of the left-wing Syriza party since 2007, and at age 33, he became the Prime Minister of Greece from 26 January 2015 to 27 August 2015.

Tsipras predicted a better future for all Europeans (presumably utilizing his ideas) addressing all those who lost in the fallout of the financial crises from 2008 to 2014. Nevertheless, the way he goes about accomplishing this is dubious.

Destructive Forces of Greed

A simple definition for greed is "a selfish, grasping desire for possession." Greed can be a very destructive force. It is not only a self-destructive force but a destructive force of others and the environment. With respect to the latter, just have a look at the destruction of the Brazilian rain forest and the exploration of the Canadian oil sands.

A very early example of the destructive force of greed is the Spanish invasion and plunder of South America. Here are some observations from the Wikipedia: The long-term effects of the arrival of the Spanish on the population of South America were simply catastrophic. While this is the case for every group of Native-Americans that encountered Europeans from the fifteenth century onwards, the Incan population suffered a dramatic and quick decline following contact. It is estimated that parts of the empire, notably the Central Andes, suffered a population decline ratio of 58:1 during the years of 1520–1571. The single greatest cause of the decimation of native populations was infectious disease. Old World Eurasian diseases, which had long been endemic on the Continent, were carried unknowingly by colonists and conquistadors. As these were new to the natives, they had no acquired immunity and suffered very high rates of death. More died of disease than any army or armed conflict. As the Inca did not have as strong a writing tradition as the Aztec or Maya, it is difficult for historians to estimate population decline or any events after conquest.

An outbreak of smallpox, believed to be hemorrhagic, reached the Andes in 1524. While numbers are unavailable, Spanish records indicate that the population was so devastated by diseases that they could hardly resist the foreign forces. Beyond the devastation of the local populations by disease, they suffered considerable enslavement, pillaging, and destruction from warfare. The Spanish took thousands of women from the local natives to use as servants and concubines. As Pizarro and his men took over portions of South America, they plundered and enslaved countless people. Some local populations entered into vassalage willingly, to defeat the Inca. Native groups such as the Huanca, Cañari, and Chachapoya fought alongside the Spanish as they opposed Inca rule. The basic policy of the Spanish towards local populations was that voluntary vassalage would yield safety and coexistence, while continued resistance would result in more deaths and destruction. Another significant effect on the people in South America was the spread of Christianity. As Pizarro and the Spanish subdued the continent and brought it under their control, they forcefully converted many to Christianity, claiming to have educated them in the ways of the "one true religion." With the depopulation of the local populations along with the capitulation of the Inca Empire, the Spanish missionary work after colonization began was able to continue unimpeded. It took just a generation for the entire continent to be under Christian influence.

In more modern times, we experienced the destructive greed of Nazi strife for Lebensraum (living space). Lebensraum was an ideological element of Nazism, which advocated Germany's territorial expansion into Eastern Europe, justified by the need for agricultural land in order to maintain the town-and-country balance, upon which depended the moral health of the German people. In practice, during the war, the Nazi policy Generalplan Ost (Master Plan East) was to kill, deport, or enslave the Polish, Ukrainian, Russian and other Slavic populations and other peoples living there considered racially inferior to the Germans and to repopulate Eastern Europe with Germanic people to achieve Lebensraum. The populations of cities were to be exterminated by starvation, thus creating an agricultural surplus that would feed Germany, and thereby allow political replacement by and re-population with a German upper class. The eugenics of Lebensraum explicitly assumed the racial superiority of Germans as an Aryan master race (Herrenvolk), who, by virtue of their superiority (physical, mental, genetic) had the right to displace any people they deemed to be Untermenschen (sub-humans) of inferior racial stock. (Source: Wikipedia)

Land-grabbing was not an exclusive action by the Nazis, though. Russia's occupation and annexation of the Crimean Peninsula in February and March 2014 have plunged Europe into one of its gravest crises since the end of the Cold War. Despite analogies to Munich in 1938, however, Russia's invasion of this Ukrainian region is at once a replay and an escalation of tactics that the Kremlin has used for the past two decades to maintain its influence across the domains of the former Soviet Union. Since the early 1990s, Russia has either directly supported or contributed to the emergence of four breakaway ethnic regions in Eurasia: Transnistria, a self-declared state in Moldova on a strip of land between the Dniester River and Ukraine; Abkhazia, on Georgia's Black Sea coast; South Ossetia, in northern Georgia; and, to a lesser degree, Nagorno-Karabakh, a landlocked mountainous region in southwestern Azerbaijan that declared its independence under Armenian protection following a brutal civil war. Moscow's meddling has created so-called frozen conflicts in these states, in which the splinter territories remain beyond the control of the central governments and the local de facto authorities enjoy Russian protection and influence. (Source: Foreign Affairs, May/June 2014 Issue)

Business leaders are greedy by nature, mainly to maximize their profits, and, sometimes, their greed leads to fraud. One of the biggest fraud cases in US history happened with Bernard L. Madoff Investment Securities LLC. Bernie Madoff dreamt up a Ponzi scheme that cheated investors out of an estimated $64.8 billion. The way he worked this is by paying huge dividends as well as redemptions out of monies invested by his clients rather than the earnings on his investments. This scheme can work only for as long as new capital is being constantly invested, otherwise, payout shortages will catch up. This is what happened to Bernie when he was struggling to meet $7 billion in redemptions, while at the same time planning to pay out $173 million in bonuses two months early. When his sons asked him how he intended to pay these bonuses while struggling to meet his clients' redemptions expectations. Madoff told them that he was finished and had absolutely nothing left. His investment fund was "just one big lie" and "basically one big Ponzi scheme." His sons reported him to the federal authorities, and he was arrested.

Most likely the largest accumulation of wealth in the world belongs to the Roman Catholic Church. Many smart people have wracked their brains and resources to determine even a ballpark figure for its total wealth – all in vain, since not even insiders know the answer. The Church has worldwide real estate holdings, art objects whose value can never even be estimated, and investments in the trillions of dollars.

As far as greed is concerned, the Roman Catholic Church makes the Madoff Ponzi scheme look like small potatoes. It has been said that the wealth of the Roman Catholic Church could easily and permanently eliminate poverty in the world.

On a microscale compared to the above examples, there are also personal examples of greed that can be destructive: overeating, drinking alcohol to excess, amassing risky investments, heirs' inheritance jealousies, the overpowering desire for vengeance, misuse of power that invites assassination, and so on. Imagine the destructive force involved.

Killing the Leader

Killing the leader seems like the only solution to a problem for some people. Take the case of Julius Caesar: he was a renowned Roman statesman and general. His victories in the Gallic Wars extended Rome's territory to the English Channel and the Rhine. He conducted the first invasion of Britain. When he was ordered to step down from his military command, he refused. Instead, he crossed the Rubicon with a legion and illegally entered Roman Italy under arms. Civil war resulted, and Caesar was in an unrivaled position of power and influence, and assumed control of government. He was eventually proclaimed "dictator in perpetuity." However, the underlying political conflicts still existed, and on the Ides of March 44 BC, Caesar was assassinated by a group of rebellious senators. There is no doubt that Caesar was a great leader, but being a great leader is never a guaranty against assassination when jealous factions are involved.

Jesus Christ was a great leader, and as all leaders do, he attracted enemies. After raising Lazarus from the dead, his last major miracle, the tension between him and the authorities increased, and they conspired to kill him. The chief priests would have had no problem finding him, but Judas Iscariot offered to deliver Jesus unto them for payment, and they paid him thirty pieces of silver. Judas then sought an opportunity to betray Jesus. His opportunity came after Jesus went to Gethsemane for some final prayers. Judas arrived the next morning with a multitude from the chief priests and elders of the people, bearing swords and staves, to arrest Jesus. They took him first to Annas, the high priest Caiaphas's father-in-law, and then to Caiaphas to be interrogated, i.e., asked if he is indeed the Messiah, but Jesus was vague with his answers. Then they took him to the Roman governor Pontius Pilate, and requested Pilate to judge and condemn Jesus, accusing Jesus of claiming to be the King of the Jews, but Pilate is extremely reluctant to do so. When Pilate realizes that Jesus is Galilean, coming under the jurisdiction of Herod Antipas, he sends him to Herod to be tried. Jesus is even less responsive to Herod's questions, and Herod returns Jesus to Pilate. Pilate calls together the Jewish elders and announces that he has not found Jesus guilty. Pilate suggests that they follow a prevailing Passover custom allowing one prisoner chosen by the crowd to be freed. The crowd, persuaded by the elders, chooses to release Barabbas, a murderer, and crucify Jesus.

And thus, another great leader was killed, regardless of his popularity.

Jesus was not the only religious leader who was killed – look at the many popes who were killed, starting with the first pope, Saint Peter, who was also crucified. Most of the popes who were killed during the first millennium AD ended up as martyrs. One interesting killing is that of Pope John VIII. He was assassinated (clubbed to death) in 882 AD, presumably because of his collapse of the papal treasury, or his friendliness towards the Byzantines, or his failure to resolve Italy's Muslim problem. According to Patrick Madrid, author of *Pope Fiction*, a book about the legend of Pope Joan, Pope John VIII may have been the origin of the Pope Joan legend because of his weak and effeminate personality, which gave rise to the legend. If there is any truth to the legend, it would not preclude a reason for killing him. More recently, Pope John Paul I died in September 1978, thirty-three days after his election, leaving questions in the minds of some people. Discrepancies of the Vatican's account of events surrounding his death gave rise to a number of conspiracy theories, some associated with the Vatican Bank, that still exist to this day. Nevertheless, the papal occupation is much less fatal than it used to be.

Disagreements with powerful political or military

leaders often lead to assassination attempts and sometimes to successful assassinations, as cited above in the case of Julius Caesar. The twentieth century saw quite a number of assassination attempts and many dozens of assassinations. Even the execution of the Russian Tsar Nicholas II by the Bolsheviks, and the execution of Benito Mussolini by Italian communists, can be classified as assassinations. Certainly the killings of US President John F. Kennedy, his brother, US Senator Robert F. Kennedy, and Martin Luther King, Jr., the American Baptist minister, activist, humanitarian and leader in the African-American Civil Rights Movement, along with Egyptian President Anwar Sadat, and Pierre Laporte, Deputy Premier and Minister of Labor of the Canadian Province of Quebec, were outright assassinations.

Of all the assassination attempts during the twentieth century, the more than two dozen attempts on the life of German Chancellor Adolf Hitler must rank as number one. The last assassination attempt, on 20 July 1944, is one of the most interesting, because Erwin Rommel, the famed "Desert Fox" was the first active-duty field marshal gave his support to the plot. Rommel had an international reputation as a humane[*] and professional officer. He ignored orders to kill

---

[*] It is interesting how an officer who orders his soldiers to kill the enemy can obtain a "humane" reputation, but Rommel had it.

Jewish soldiers, civilians, and other captured commandos. Nevertheless, although Rommel felt that he had to "come to the rescue of Germany," he thought killing Hitler would make Hitler a martyr. He wanted Hitler arrested and hauled before a court-martial to answer for his crimes. Rommel was not directly involved in resistance operations, but he had explicit knowledge of the plot to kill Hitler and did not inform him.

On 17 July 1944, Rommel's staff car was strafed by a Spitfire in France, and Rommel was hospitalized with major head injuries. Three days later, the assassination plot failed, Hitler survived, and he ordered that those responsible should be "hanged like cattle."[*] Many conspirators committed suicide, either prior to their trial or prior to their execution. Hitler was so furious he ordered Heinrich Himmler, the leader of the Gestapo, to round up all the conspirators and their relatives. Himmler complied, and more than 7,000 people were arrested, of whom 4,980 were executed. One of the conspirators admitted, under gruesome torture, that Erwin Rommel knew of the assassination plot. Hitler, however, recognized that having the popular hero branded and executed as a traitor would cause a major uproar in Germany, so he gave Rommel the choice of committing suicide rather

---

[*] I have never heard of cattle being hanged, unless after slaughter.

than turn him over to the People's Court. Rommel knew that being tried by the People's Court was tantamount to a death sentence in any case, so he agreed to the suicide option, providing his family was left alone. Hitler agreed, and Rommel was buried with full military honors. His involvement in the conspiracy never came out until after the war.

Hanging leaders seems to have been popular right into the middle of the twentieth century. Even the Allies of World War II opted for hanging Nazi criminals. Ten prominent members of the military and political leadership of Nazi Germany were executed by hanging on 16 October 1946, shortly after the conclusion of the Nuremberg trials. Herrmann Göring was also scheduled to be hanged but committed suicide the night before.

Göring was the commander-in-chief of the German Air Force from 1935 until the final days of World War II. In 1940, he was at his peak as minister in charge of the German economy in the build-up to the war, and Hitler promoted him to the rank of *Reichsmarschall*, a rank senior to all other military commanders. In 1941, Hitler designated him as his successor and deputy in all his offices. But when the German Air Force failed to stop the Allied bombing of German cities and failed to resupply German forces trapped near Stalingrad, Göring's influence with Hitler was reduced. Then, when Göring was informed on 22 April 1945 that Hitler intended to commit suicide, he sent a telegram to Hitler requesting to assume control of the German Reich. Hitler considered this request an act of treason and removed Göring from all his positions, expelled him from the Nazi party, and ordered his arrest. That's the thanks Herrmann Göring got from Adolf Hitler for trying to be helpful after the Führer's planned suicide.

A leader being assassinated, committing suicide, or dying of natural causes, every time this happens, we are short one leader. Fortunately, we have enough leaders available to replace the loss. However, when we lose a beloved leader like John F. Kennedy (JFK), the loss becomes more acute, and we are overcome by a great sadness. The reason behind JFK's assassination is still a mystery. He had made powerful enemies, of course, but who of them would have wanted to have him killed. At least eight conceivable conspiracy-to-assassinate theories still exist at present. Some theorists believe that Lyndon B. Johnson (LBJ) had the best motive to have JFK killed. Apparently, Madeline Duncan Brown, LBJ's former mistress, stated a few times that LBJ told her on 21 November 1963, the night before JFK got assassinated, "after tomorrow, the Kennedy boys will never make a fool of me again." LBJ benefitted by JFK's death, of course, but it is hard to believe that he would have stooped to have JFK killed.

A more likely theory involves Fidel Castro. Castro probably believed that JFK was behind assassination attempts against him. Even LBJ said, "I'll tell you something about Kennedy's murder that will rock you...Kennedy was trying to get Castro, but Castro got to him first." Castro was upset, of course, over the invasion at the Bay of Pigs in Cuba, and over the forced withdrawal of Russian missiles after the October 1962 crisis. The latter also angered the Russian Premier Nikita Khrushchev, and one conspirator theory has it that the KGB may have been involved in JFK's assassination.

Another theory claims that J. Edgar Hoover, Director of the FBI, had information about a plot to assassinate JFK thirteen days before it happened and did nothing about it. It was well known that Hoover was no fan of the Kennedys. The CIA also had motive to become involved in JFK's assassination, because two years previously JFK degraded the CIA over the Bay of Pigs fiasco. Even though JFK said that air strikes were not vital, which doomed the invasion, he was intent on blaming the CIA for the failure, and several CIA officials handed in their resignations.

Another conspirator theory involves the American Mafia. Many angry mobsters were unhappy with the way JFK's brother Robert F. Kennedy was prosecuting Mafia chieftains. The theorists believe that Sam Giancana and Carlos Marcello may have masterminded JFK's assassination. Giancana's girlfriend Judith Exner was reportedly also JFK's mistress, which may have given Giancana one more reason to conspire to kill JFK.

Nevertheless, the Warren Commission, which was established by LBJ on 29 November 1963 to investigate the assassination of JFK, ignored all assassination-conspiracy theories and concluded that Lee Harvey Oswald acted alone.

Four-and-a-half years later, Robert F. Kennedy (RFK), JFK's brother, was assassinated, which presents another mystery. As with JFK, RFK assassination-conspiracy theories surfaced as well but never reached the same proportions as with JFK. The Palestinian perpetrator, Sirhan Sirhan, still jailed, who could dispel such theories is not talking.

Well, as stated in the beginning, **killing the leader** seems to be the only solution to a problem for some people. Leaders know this and try to take precautions. US presidents have the Secret Service people to protect them; UK prime ministers have Metropolitan police and Special Forces; Hitler had the Schutzstaffel (SS); Joseph Stalin had the People's Comissariat for Internal Affairs, or the NKVD; and so on.

Millions, well into billions, of dollars are spent each year to protect powerful leaders from getting assassinated. Yet, leaders still get frequently killed, because some deranged people think this is the only way to correct a wrong.

State versus Religion

Most people in the world endorse some kind of religion that sustains their spirit and belief in this and, perhaps, a future life. Even when an atheistic state like Bolshevik Russia banned religions, it could never eradicate them, because people are too much in need of a religion, although less so in our times than a few hundred years back.

Take Japan as an example of what happened a few hundred years ago: Although Japan had already traded with the outside world for several decades during the seventeenth century, the ruling shogun Tokugawa Iemitsu abruptly expelled all foreigners in 1635. He also threatened foreigners who tried to enter Japan illegally, or anyone who practiced Christianity, with the death penalty. The government would ask people on the Religious Terror Watch List to step on a picture of Jesus Christ, to prove they were not Christians. Those who refused were tortured, and if that failed, killed. The ban lasted for over two-hundred years to prevent the influence of Christianity, which was brought into the country by radicalized Catholic missionaries. It finally ended in 1853, when the

American Commodore Mathew Perry fired several cannons at Japan, forcing the country to trade with the outside world.

During the sixteenth century, England had its own problems with the Roman Catholic Church. In 1534, King Henry VIII separated the English Church from Rome. He wanted an annulment of his marriage to Catherine of Aragon to marry Anne Boleyn. When Pope Clement VII refused, Henry took the position of Supreme Head of the Church of England to assure the annulment. He was excommunicated by Pope Paul III.

In 1536–40 Henry VIII engaged in the Dissolution of the Monasteries, which controlled much of the richest land. He disbanded monasteries, priories, convents and friaries in England, Wales, and Ireland, appropriated their income, disposed of their assets, and provided pensions for the former residents. The properties were sold to pay for the wars. Bernard[*] argues: The dissolution of the monasteries in the late 1530s was one of the most revolutionary events in English history.[†]

Advancing to the twentieth century, it is also interesting to note how religion was treated in Nazi Germany: In 1933, prior to the annexation of Austria into Germany, the population of Germany was

---

[*] G.W. Bernard, "The Dissolution of the Monasteries," History (2011)
[†] Source: Wikipedia

approximately 67% Protestant and 33% Catholic; Jews made up less than 1% of the population. A census in 1939, six years into the Nazi era and incorporating the annexation of mostly Catholic Austria into Germany, indicates that 54% considered themselves Protestant, 40% Catholic, 3.5% self-identified as "gottgläubig" (lit. "believers in god", often described as predominately creationist and deistic), and 1.5% as non-religious. There was some diversity of personal views among the Nazi leadership as to the future of religion in Germany. Anti-Church radicals included Hitler's Personal Secretary Martin Bormann, Minister for Propaganda Joseph Goebbels, Neo-Pagan Nazi Philosopher Alfred Rosenberg, and Neo-Pagan Occultist Reichsführer-SS Heinrich Himmler.

Some Nazis, such as Hans Kerrl, who served as Hitler's Minister for Church Affairs, believed Christianity could be Nazified into "Positive Christianity", by renouncing its Jewish origins, the Old Testament and Apostle's Creed, and holding Hitler as a new "Messiah." Under the Gleichschaltung process, Hitler attempted to create a unified Protestant Reich Church from Germany's 28 existing Protestant churches. The plan failed. Persecution of the Catholic Church in Germany followed the Nazi takeover. Hitler moved quickly to eliminate Political Catholicism. Amid harassment of the Church, the Reich concordat treaty with the Vatican was signed in 1933, and promised to respect Church autonomy. Hitler routinely disregarded the Concordat, closing all Catholic institutions whose functions were not strictly religious.

Clergy, nuns, and lay leaders were targeted, with thousands of arrests over the ensuing years. Smaller religious minorities such as the Jehovah's Witnesses and Bahá'í Faith were banned in Germany, while the eradication of Judaism by the genocide of its adherents was attempted. The Salvation Army, Christian Saints, and Seventh Day Adventist Church all disappeared from Germany, while astrologers, healers, and fortune tellers were banned. The small pagan "German Faith Movement", which worshipped the sun and seasons, supported the Nazis. Many historians believed that Hitler and the Nazis intended to eradicate Christianity in Germany after attaining victory in the war.[*]

However, the Nazis were unsuccessful in their attempt to Nazify religions, just as the Bolshevists were unsuccessful in banning religions.

During the Stalinist period, the Russian regime destroyed church buildings, or put them to secular use, executed clergy, prohibited publications of religious materials, and persecuted members of religious groups – eventually, all to no avail. More recently, as per the Wikipedia, according to a poll by the Russian Public

---

[*] Source: Wikipedia

Opinion Research Center, 63% of respondents considered themselves Russian Orthodox, 6% of respondents considered themselves Muslim, and less than 1% considered themselves either Buddhist, Catholic, Protestant or Jewish. Another 12% said they believe in God, but did not practice any religion, and 16% said they are non-believers.

The USA practiced its own exclusion during the nineteenth century. After an explosion of immigration from China during the gold rush, which undercut American laborers and increased the use of addictive drugs, Congress passed the Chinese Exclusion Act in 1882, intended to halt Chinese immigration to the USA. Then, in 1924, when Japanese immigrants started to gain a foothold in the USA, the Immigration Act banned *all* East Asian Immigration. However, when China and America joined forces during World War II, it became awkward to enforce a discriminatory immigration policy, and the act was repealed in 1943.

The Puritan separatists, who were expelled from England because they wanted to worship God on their own terms, without joining the Church of England, were forced to live in Holland for a while, and eventually negotiated with the Crown to colonize Massachusetts in 1620 – evidently a win-win solution.

We still have much opposition to religious freedom in the world. For example, in Albania, during the totalitarian regime installed after World War II, religions were banned altogether, and many clergy and believers were tried and some executed. Foreign Roman Catholic priests, monks, and nuns were expelled. Albania was the only country that ever officially banned religion. This situation has more recently improved, but is still far from perfect as far as religious freedom is concerned.

Another example is when the Khmer Rouge attempted to eliminate Cambodia's cultural heritage, including its religion, particularly Theravada Buddhism. In the process, its followers killed about 1.7 million people. A mere 3,000 monks survived. There had been 60,000 monks previously.[*]

We have also thirteen countries that still experience physical violent incidents over conversions from one religion to another. Ten of these are Muslim countries: Afghanistan, Bahrain, Bangladesh, Jordan, Comoros, Egypt, Nigeria, Pakistan, Somalia, and Syria; the other three countries are India, Mongolia, and Nepal. There are also quite a number of countries where religion-related terrorist groups enact violence that result in many injuries and deaths.

You may wonder where some of the anti-religion sentiment comes from. Well, some widespread antipathy to religions is spawned by renowned people

---

[*] Source: Wikipedia

who speak out against religion. Here are some examples: David Hume (1711-1776) wrote that human reason is wholly inadequate to make any assumptions about the divine. Thomas Paine (1737-1809) wrote a scathing critique on religion in the *Age of Reason*: "All national institutions of churches, whether Jewish, Christian, or Muslim, appear to me no other than human inventions set up to terrify and enslave mankind, and monopolize power and profit." Karl Marx (1818-1883) was well known for his anti-religious views. He called religion "the opium of the people." Friedrich Nietzsche (1844-1900) wrote several critical texts on religion. John Dewey (1859-1952) believed that neither religion nor metaphysics could provide legitimate moral or social values, though scientific empiricism could. Richard Dawkins (born 1941) criticizes the belief in the divine. Christopher Hitchens (1949-2011) wrote *God Is Not Great: How Religion Poisons Everything*. Steven Pinker (born 1954) believes religion incites violence. Sam Harris (born 1967) says that religious moderation provides cover for dangerous fundamentalism. Then we have Vladimir Lenin, the Soviet leader from 1917 to 1924, who believed all religions to be the organs of bourgeois reaction, used to stupefy the working class.

In the final analysis, though, religion cannot be banned or eliminated. Billions of people in the world depend on some kind of religion for their mental peace and security. It is understandable that governments want to function without interference from religious groups, but to ban or eliminate religions to accomplish is not the answer.

The Group of Twenty-Two

The Group of Twenty-Two is a living group of twenty-two people who are the wisest[*] in the world, regardless of power, fame, or intelligence quotient, and each member's wisdom is far reaching.

This new group has its origin in my book *Human Traits & Follies*, published February 2015. I have requested from several of my friends and relatives to give me nominees for this group, and reasons for nominating them.[†]

My own nominees are Queen Elizabeth II, Pope

----

[*] Wikipedia definition: Wisdom or sapience is the ability to think and act using knowledge, experience, understanding, common sense, and insight. Wisdom has been regarded as one of four cardinal virtues; and as a virtue, it is a habit or disposition to perform the action with the highest degree of adequacy under any given circumstance, and to avoid wrongdoing. This implies a possession of knowledge or the seeking of knowledge to apply to the given circumstance. This involves an understanding of people, objects, events, situations, and the willingness as well as the ability to apply perception, judgement, and action in keeping with the understanding of what is the optimal course of action. It often requires control of one's emotional reactions (the "passions") so that the universal principle of reason prevails to determine one's action. In short, wisdom is a disposition to find the truth coupled with an optimum judgement as to what actions should be taken.

[†] The date when this chapter was written, 27 June 2016, is important to note because nominees must still be alive.

Francis, and Vladimir Putin. I will explain the reasons for my choices shortly. Also, in my book *Human Traits & Follies* I suggested Angela Merkel as a possible nominee, but as my friend Jim Lampard pointed out to me, Angela Merkel's actions cast doubt on her wisdom, although he concurs with me on Queen Elizabeth II and Pope Francis. Here are Jim's comments on Angela Merkel:

> Her stance on the eurozone and the mass acceptance of refugees will not be seen as wise. While Merkel didn't create the eurozone her resistance to reforms that would make it workable such as letting Europe issue bonds, banking integration and debt restructuring cannot be seen as wise. The eurozone has created a two tier EU [European Union] and imposed austerity on many countries that is leading to a lost generation, mass unemployment, and giving rise to radical parties that want to destroy the EU. The mass acceptance of refugees has fueled these same forces and even brought the radical right to within a hair of power in Austria and growing in Germany. The refugee crisis combined with austerity are putting great pressure on the EU; witness the rise of leave forces in France and Netherlands to name just two.

Jim Lampard nominated the following as a good addition to the list: George Soros – he's not just a great investor, but he's behind many great causes, including the transition of Eastern Europe from communism; Ben Bernanke, who served two terms as chairman of the US Federal Reserve, and who got the world through the financial crisis; US ex-President Jimmy Carter; and US President Barack Obama. Jim says Obama is leading the US in a different and to his mind better foreign policy, and too bad he has been hampered by an intransigent Republican Party; Obama would have done many great things.

When Obama was first elected in 2008, I was simply elated. I thought he had wisdom, intellect, and a fresh approach. However, I lost some of my fervor over the last eight years, but I still agree with Jim.

Jim also nominated the English scientist and philosopher Richard Dawkins, who wrote a book called *The God Delusion*. Some people may disagree with this nomination because Richard Dawkins is an atheist, but this would be a poor reason to eliminate him. I happen to disagree with the nomination because of Richard Dawkins's faulty reasoning, which I had pointed out in my book *Conclusions Volume I*.

As three additions, Jim Lampard has nominated Stephen Hawking, the theoretical physicist and cosmologist; Aung San Suu Kyi,[*] who has led Burma to democracy; and Hu Jintao, the Chinese leader from 2008-2013, whose peaceful reform and development have been far superior with less human cost than the radical changes that occurred with the breakup of the USSR. Jim adds the following reasons, quoting the Wikipedia: Hu advocated for China's peaceful development, pursuing soft power and a business-oriented approach to diplomacy. Through Hu's tenure, China's influence in Africa, Latin America, and other developing countries has increased.

My granddaughter Samantha has nominated Deepak Chopra, an Indian American author, public speaker, alternative medicine advocate, and prominent figure in the New Age movement. Her reasons for the nomination: His perspectives on humanity and energy and his philosophy can free people, if they so choose, from their metaphorical materialistic shackles, and enable everyone to live the most fulfilling, connected life possible. I think he is a very wise man.

My granddaughter Megan has nominated the Dalai Lama, and Jim Lampard agrees with her. Jim Lampard's reason is that as spiritual leader of a branch of Tibetan Buddhism the Dalai Lama has been taught the wisdom of the ages and leads while his people are

* I have given Aung San Suu Kyi a tribute in my book *Conclusions Volume II.*

oppressed by the Chinese.

My grandson Garett has nominated Bill Gates and Warren Buffett. Garett did not give any reasons for his nominations.

Garett's friend Vickie Hon has nominated Donald Trump; she gave the following reasons: Even though some of [Mr. Trump's] comments may be harsh, I feel that he is wise because he knows how to run a successful business and he knows how to captivate the audiences with his persona.

My sister Birgit has also nominated Donald Trump.

My friend Wayne Wilson has nominated Jimmy Carter, US ex-president, and Stephen Hawking.

I'm now obliged to mention that I was not impressed with the way Jimmy Carter handled the Iran hostage crisis. However, I was certainly impressed with his wisdom since his term in office. In 2002, he was even awarded the Nobel Peace Prize.

My friend David Munro has nominated Warren Buffet, Donald Trump, and me. For my nomination, my wisdom is not only questionable; what disqualifies me is this: if I had any acceptable wisdom it would not be far-reaching enough.

My friend Andrea Schmelcher has nominated Warren Buffett. Her reasons are: He's got some great quotes on investing, and on life, and his belief that the rich are overcompensated has resulted in him being a philanthropist.

My sister Waltraud has nominated Benjamin Netanyahu with these reasons: First, he always steps out into the most challenging situations; second, Benjamin and his wife Sarah hold hands when they go on business trips together; third, he has the most dashing personality. [No wisdom examples, though.]

My daughter Nancy nominated Rick Steves. She likes his unbiased comments on European travelogues. She also nominated British ex-Prime Minister David Cameron, because he was the most reasonable and calm person in the Brexit affair, and Angela Merkel. She says about Merkel: I know that people don't like the number of refugees she let into Germany, but in other ways she's done a good job in trying to keep Europe as stable as possible. In addition, Nancy nominated Prince William, Queen Elizabeth II's grandson. Nancy says: I know he's young yet, but from what I've seen of him I think that he gets along with people very well. He tries to find a solution rather than getting into an argument with them. He seems to have inherited the common sense that the Queen has.

My cousin and friend Bernie Jeske nominated the 97-year-old icon Billy Graham, ordained as a Southern Baptist minister.

My friend Mario Richard's wife, Francine,

nominated the philanthropist Bill Gates, co-founder of Microsoft, and Craig Kielburger, co-founder of Free the Children.

My friends Fred and Barbara Melnyk also nominated Bill Gates, as well as Warren Buffett and Barack Obama. In addition, they nominated Mark Zuckerberg and Melala Yousafzai. Zuckerberg is a programmer, Internet entrepreneur, philanthropist, and the chairman, chief executive, and co-founder of the social networking website Facebook; and Yousafzai is a Pakistani activist for female education, and the youngest-ever Nobel Prize laureate.

My friend Pamela Sigvaldason sent me the following email: I agree with all of *your* choices [Angela Merkel, Queen Elizabeth II, Pope Francis, and Vladimir Putin] and Megan's too, which caused me some grief as my initial candidates were in this group. So my choice is Condoleezza Rice. As you know she was the 66th US Secretary of State. I believe that she meets the criteria for the group as she had the wisdom and courage to state her views on Iraq at a time that it was not necessarily a popular viewpoint. She is a product of the segregated school system and despite her color and sex has been able to be recognized and valued for her wisdom.

My friend Jim Clarke has nominated Noam Chomsky, the American linguist, philosopher, cognitive scientist, historian, logician, social critic, and political activist; Fidel Castro, the Cuban politician and revolutionary who governed the Republic of Cuba as Prime Minister from 1959 to 1976 and then as President from 1976 to 2008; and Jean Chrétien, the Canadian politician and statesman who served as the 20th Prime Minister of Canada from November 4, 1993 to December 12, 2003. Jim's reasons for his nominations are as follows: Noam Chomsky brings to the free world a look into the mirror. His insights into the many illusions that have been created by business and government for the good of all are enlightening to say the least. He peels back the onion and gets to the facts formulating opinions on right and wrong. Regarding Fidel Castro, one doesn't have to agree with the politics, however, Fidel "Stayed the Course." His resolve was unquestionable. It is only the people of Cuba that should judge their circumstance; however, they have more doctors, dentists, and educators per capita than any country in the free world. [It is] great to have good teeth, even if the food is poor in quality. Regarding Jean Chrétien, [he is] one of the few Prime Ministers that led for the people, without being left wing in his politics. He was respected on the world stage and brought a respect to Canadian ways. He was not so far left that business could rebel. Canada grew under his leadership.

My daughter Diana has nominated Brandon Stanton, who is an American photographer and blogger; he is most known as the founder of Humans of New York, a popular photojournalistic work; and Ryan Holmes, who is a Canadian computer programmer and internet entrepreneur; he is best known as the founder and CEO of Hootsuite, a social media management tool for businesses.

Diana's friend Rob Hatchwell has submitted four nominations: Catherine Austin Fitts, the president of Solari, Inc., also a reoccurring guest on the overnight radio program Coast to Coast AM; David Icke, the English writer and public speaker; Kevin Annett, writer and anthropologist, who was a priest of the United Church of Canada and is best known as Louie Lawless; and Joel D. Wallach, M.S., D.V.M. and N.D. who is a veterinarian and naturopath.

My nephew David Hoffmann has nominated the Dalai Lama as his first choice, Queen Elizabeth II as his second choice, and Angela Merkel as his third choice. In the case of Angela Merkel, he offered the comment that he only knows about her from the news, "but she seems really on top of things."

My friend Ed Lee has nominated Warren Buffett; also Mark Carney, the Canadian economist who currently serves as Governor of the Bank of England and Chairman of the G20's Financial Stability Board, and earlier as the Governor of the Bank of Canada.

My friend Ron Abraham has also nominated Mark Carney.

My friend Tara Petersen has nominated Pope Francis. She asserts that he is truly selfless and very inclusive; given the world times, he is very wise.

My friend Doug Gillis has also nominated Pope Francis. He says Pope Francis appears to be an honest, trustworthy, frugal, humble, and sincere individual, and it does not appear that his sole mission is to lie and steal from parishioners in an attempt to advance his church, as all other religious leaders do.

My Friend Bob Lynn nominated David Johnston, the current Governor General of Canada; he has been involved with politics, public service, moderating political debates, and chairing commissions in both federal and provincial spheres; in a speech delivered 14 August 2011, Johnston attracted media attention by criticizing the legal profession. Bob Lynn thinks Mr. Johnston is one of the wisest men in Canada. Bob also agrees with the nomination of Queen Elizabeth II, who appointed David Johnston.

Last but not least, what are my reasons for nominating Queen Elizabeth II? What can I say? This woman has dealt admirably with personal problems as well as with national and international problems, and she has done this with very little unpleasantness since

6 February 1952 – for over sixty-four years!

Pope Francis I nominated because I like his ability to find a balance between his religious canons and contemporary demands, which definitely requires a lot of wisdom.

Vladimir Putin I nominated because he does not lose his cool in the face of all the criticism he receives and must endure. Few people in the West like him, but I think he is liked, for the most part, by his fellow Russians. Jim Lampard disagrees with my nomination of him; he calls Putin a great tactician, an opportunist, and quite ruthless, but not wise. Jim says he would definitely put Putin on the most influential list. However, I'm not sure about that, because Putin is not very influential with Westerners. Nevertheless, in light of Jim's objections, I think my reason for nominating Putin may be too weak.

In addition, I would also like to nominate Dan Cruickshank. Dan impressed me with his wisdom during his commentaries for the television series *Around the World in 80 Treasures* – a quest for mankind's greatest achievements.

Jim Lampard had also suggested that perhaps a really wise judge would be another good addition to the list. Okay, Jim, how about Judge Aaron Persky, the American judge sitting on the Superior Court of California, County of Santa Clara? In 2016, Persky received international media attention and widespread criticism for sentencing Brock Allen Turner, a 20-year-old Stanford student convicted of three felony counts of sexual assault, to six months in jail and three years of probation. Nancy Brewer, a retired Santa Clara County assistant public defender, described Persky as "respected by both prosecutors and defenders" and viewed as "a fair judge who is not soft on crime or someone who gives lenient sentences." Brewer said that Persky "carefully evaluated the evidence and did what he thought was a fair and appropriate sentence in the case" based upon the Santa Clara County Probation Department's presentence investigation report. [Source: Wikipedia]

There must be many millions of people who would qualify to become members of The Group of Twenty-Two, and there is no doubt that at least some of those nominated by my friends, my relatives, and me would be eligible for membership in this Group, but our nominations may not necessarily be admitted without stricter evaluations. After all, to be one of the wisest in the world is quite an attainment.

These nominations convey an interesting story about us as well as about the people we nominated.

The Meaning of Life

Here is an excerpt of a definition from the Wikipedia for the meaning of life: The meaning of life as we perceive it is derived from our philosophical and religious contemplation of, and scientific inquiries about existence, social ties, consciousness, and happiness. Many other issues are also involved, such as symbolic meaning, ontology, value, purpose, ethics, good and evil, free will, and the existence of one or multiple gods, conceptions of God, the soul, and the afterlife. Scientific contributions focus primarily on describing related empirical facts about the universe, exploring the context and parameters concerning the 'how' of life. Science also studies and can provide recommendations for the pursuit of well-being and a related conception of morality. An alternative, humanistic approach poses the question, "What is the meaning of my life?"

For animals, excluding human beings, and plants the meaning of life is simply to feed their bodies and reproduce themselves. For human beings, in addition to feeding their bodies and reproducing themselves, the meaning of life takes on more expanded and deeper aspects. Human beings also like to feed their minds, their spirits, their vanities, and their greed, and, perhaps, attain a life hereafter.

Human babies are taught a language to deal with these expanded aspects, and the language itself is expanded during school days. Then, they are taught how to behave themselves in the social environment, and, later in life, they are taught how to deal with and evaluate any deeper aspects they may encounter during their lives. Hopefully, as far as their parents are concerned, all these instructions will help to create usefulness and a deeper meaning in their lives. Nevertheless, in the end, the meaning of life may not extend beyond that of more primitive animals.

Human beings like to think that their highly developed brain deserves a deeper meaning of life than just feeding and procreating the body. Surely such a marvelous brain deserves a better meaning of life – even to live forever. This is one of the foremost vanities of human beings, and from this vanity flow all other vanities and arrogances of self-importance. The Preacher, I think, had it right when he told us *all is vanity*. Greed also feeds our vanities; thus, even greed becomes part of our vanities. All is vanity!

Still, who can blame us for being in love with our marvelous minds? When we look at our scientific achievements, this love affair is quite understandable.

Yet, a large part of our scientific achievements is designed to kill our fellow human beings. Every time a war occurs, major strides forward are achieved to kill the maximum number of people.

Take Alfred Nobel, the Swedish scientist who invented dynamite, as an example. It would be difficult to determine how many millions, if not billions, of lives his inventions have cost. Alfred Nobel also owned Bofors AB, a major manufacturer of cannons and other armaments. After he read a premature obituary of his life, which criticized him for making huge profits from the sale of arms, he donated his fortune to found the Nobel Prizes. This action, then, became the real meaning of his life, even though his other actions were designed to ruin the lives of his fellows, which, I'm sure, he would not have considered the meaning of his life.

The normal scheme of things with human beings, after their initial education, is to firstly make a living, and then, if possible, accumulate wealth and, conceivably, gain power over their fellow human beings. But none of these activities may provide any of them with a meaningful life – meaningful to his or her fellow human beings. What could be a meaningful life, though, as far as our fellow human beings are concerned, is what we are able to pass on to them, whether it is knowledge or wealth, to advance the progress and well-being of future generations.

In other words, it is not what an individual achieves for him- or herself that gives a meaning to his or her life, but what he or she can contribute to promote the advance of future generations of human beings. Nevertheless, this notion may be in conflict with individual and selfish concepts of the meaning of life, especially when religious issues become involved, such as pleasing one's God or trying to achieve an afterlife. I have already stated this notion in the last verse of my poem called *The Search for Life's Meaning*, which was published in my book called *Characters*:

Then, finally, you must give all back,
Which fell into your hands along the trek:
Your possessions, your mind, and even your heart,
To give human beings a better start.
This action will be your contribution
To the cycle of life and its evolution.

Suicide as a Final Solution

Suicide was a chosen alternative to life since the earliest days of human existence. The death of Socrates is an interesting case of suicide. Socrates was put on trial in Athens for corrupting the minds of youths in Athens and impiety, i.e., not believing in the gods of the state. He was sentenced to death by drinking a mixture of poison hemlock. He could have escaped this outcome, because his followers were able to bribe the prison guards, but decided to remain and be executed. Here are some of the reasons offered why he decided to stay:

1. He believed such a flight would indicate a fear of death, which he believed no true philosopher has.
2. If he fled Athens his teaching would fare no better in another country, as he would continue questioning all he met and undoubtedly incur their displeasure.
3. Having knowingly agreed to live under the city's laws, he implicitly subjected himself to the possibility of being accused of crimes by its citizens and judged guilty by its jury. To do

otherwise would have caused him to break his "social contract" with the state, and so harm the state, an unprincipled act.

4. If he escaped at the instigation of his friends, then his friends would become liable in law.[*]

Thus, by refusing to escape, Socrates committed suicide, but his was a heroic suicide. On the other hand, the suicides of top Nazi officials, like Hitler and Goebbels, were the suicides of cowards who did not want to stick around to face the consequences of their actions. Other suicides are the result of hopelessness. For example, Herrmann Goering committed suicide after he was sentenced to hang; Ernest Hemingway committed suicide after he determined he could no longer write and was a victim of dementia; John Robarts, the 17th Premier of Ontario, committed suicide after suffering a series of debilitating strokes; these suicides, in the face of hopelessness, are understandable and take courage to carry out. However, some suicides will always remain puzzles.

One of the strangest and most puzzling suicide pacts was formed between Henriette Vogel and Heinrich von Kleist. Henriette Vogel was a married woman when she met Heinrich von Kleist in 1809. Henriette and Heinrich became fast friends because of

---

[*] See Wikipedia.

similar interests. She asked Heinrich to teach her the art of fencing as well as the art of war.

Henriette had been diagnosed with terminal cancer of the uterus. Her husband, Louis, averted her with dislike, and she began to express the wish to die. This wish is understandable. However, Heinrich von Kleist led a productive life in literature and was well respected. Therefore, his desire to commit suicide is much less understandable, and has caused considerable speculation.

By fall 1811, Henriette and Heinrich had developed a very intimate relationship, not in the passionate sense but spiritually. Heinrich, too, bore visions of suicide during his life; thus, he became an ideal partner for Henriette, and on 21 November 1811 he shot first Henriette and then himself.

In a letter to her husband, Henriette wrote: "I can no longer bear life, because it feels like an iron clamp around my heart – you can call it a sickness, a weakness, or whatever you want, I myself do not know what to call it – all I can say is that I look forward to my death as a lucky event…If I could take you all, whom I love, with me, you might all follow to the eternal, splendid union, oh, then, I would have nothing more to desire. Kleist, who will be my loyal companion in death, as he was in life, will see to my passage and will then shoot himself."

Heinrich, too, wrote a last letter – to his half-sister Ulrike: "I can't die, without, as satisfied and happy as I am with the whole world, as well as especially my dearest Ulrike, having reconciled with you. Let me take back the severe statement that is contained in the letter to the Kleists; really, you did for me not only what was in the power of a sister but what was humanly possible to save me: the truth is that on Earth I could not be helped. And now, live well: may heaven give you a death with only half the joy and ineffable serenity as mine: that is the heartiest and dearest wish that I can come up with for you. [Written in] Stimmings at Potsdam, in the morning of my death, Your Heinrich." Both letters have entered the world's literature. [The letter translations are mine.]

Heinrich's desire to die remains mysterious. It is interesting what people inscribed about them on their joint gravestone: "He lived, sang, and suffered, in troubled, difficult times; he sought death here, and found immortality." [The verse was written by Jewish poet Max Ring – translation mine] In other words, Henriette's and Heinrich's joint suicide made both of them immortal, and it is possible that this was Heinrich's intent.

Some mass suicides, in the face of hopelessness, can also be considered heroic. For example, when the Teutons and the Cimbri invaded Italy in 102 BC, they were defeated by the Roman Gaius Marius at the battle of Aquae Sextiae. A surrender condition was to turn three hundred of their married women over to the Romans. When the matrons begged the Roman consul to let them serve in the temples of Ceres and Venus and were refused and removed by the lictors, they decided to slay their children and commit suicide by strangling themselves during the night; their action passed into Roman legends as Germanic heroism.

Another heroic mass suicide happened in 73 AD, when 960 members of the Sicarii Jewish community at Masada killed each other rather than be conquered and enslaved by the Romans. Each man killed his wife and children; then the men drew lots and killed each other until the last man killed himself.

In more recent heroic history, on 1 May 1945, about a thousand residents of Demmin, Germany, committed mass suicide after the Red Army had sacked their town.

Then, we had the kamikaze (divine wind) warriors from the Empire of Japan, who were flying their aircraft into allied warships during World War II. About 3,860 of the kamikaze pilots died on their missions. The practice of suicide rather than defeat, capture, and shame was deep-rooted in the Japanese military culture, going all the way back to the samurai life, and probably considered as heroic as fighting the enemy. Compare the kamikaze warriors to modern-day suicide bombers. Can the latter terrorist tactic also be considered heroic?

Reasons for suicide, beside heroic acts, can include incurable illness, mental illness, alcoholism, drug abuse, or impulses due to stress. Common methods to terminate life include hanging, poisoning, and shooting. Suicide caused 842,000 deaths in 2013, up from 712,000 deaths in 1990, which makes it the tenth leading death cause worldwide. In addition, there are an estimated ten to twenty million non-fatal attempted suicides every year. In general, males are more likely to kill themselves than females, but females' attempted suicides are four times more common than males' attempts. Some religions consider suicide an offence towards God, whereas other religions support suicide. For example, during the samurai era in Japan suicide was respected as a means to make up for failure or as a form of protest. In India, sati, a practice that expected the Indian widow to kill herself on her husband's funeral fire, willingly or at family pressure, was eventually outlawed. Suicides and attempted suicides are no longer illegal in most Western societies, but remain a criminal offence in many countries.

One interesting development is a more open mind toward assisted euthanasia and assisted suicide.

Assisted euthanasia is when a doctor administers the means to die, and assisted suicide is when the doctor only provides the means to the patient for self-administration. Here is a list of countries that have legalized the practice as of October 2015: human euthanasia is legal in Ireland, Belgium, Colombia, the Netherlands, and Luxembourg. Assisted suicide is legal in Switzerland, Germany, Japan, Albania, Canada,[*] and in the US states of Washington, Oregon, Vermont, New Mexico, Montana, and California.

I am in favor of assisted euthanasia and assisted suicide. It is my life; I should be allowed to make my own decisions about it, not a government authority. The government-authorized professional person to

---

[*] On 6 February 2015, the Supreme Court of Canada sent a powerful message around the world. In a unanimous decision, the justices of the high court struck down the federal prohibition on physician-assisted dying (PAD), arguing the old law violates the Canadian Charter of Rights and Freedoms. This decision promises to reshape how we think about death and dying in the years to come. On 6 June 2016, the legal ban on physician-assisted dying expired. Until Canada passes a national framework, eligibility for PAD will be determined based on the Supreme Court's guidelines. In its decision, the Supreme Court decriminalized physician-assisted death for Canadians with a "grievous and irremediable" medical condition (an illness, disease, or disability) that causes enduring suffering that is intolerable to the individual. The court did not define "grievous and irremediable," but it is clearly not limited to terminal illness. Only competent, consenting adults will be allowed to access PAD. Someone who has dementia but is still competent to provide informed consent may qualify, provided their suffering is intolerable to them at the time of the request. (Source: Dying With Dignity Canada)

assist a suicide should be a qualified medical doctor. It is then up to a doctor to decide whether or not to assist a suicide. Just as a doctor would not prescribe medication for a nonexistent illness, a doctor would not assist a frivolous suicide. But a patient who is incurably ill and has unbearable pain would, at his or her request, readily get a doctor's assistance to end his or her life.

Of course, I am deliberately omitting moral and religious considerations here, because I am addressing government authority over a person's life, and the government's authority should also be free of moral and religious considerations.

Love Thy Enemy

The definition of existence in the natural world depends on atoms or energy, and in the abstract, mythical, and fictional worlds existence depends on the mind. If we accept this definition of existence, nonexistence may truly be nonexistent. Thus, we must be careful when expressing nonexistence, because when objects, or rather concepts, do not exist in the natural world, they may well exist in the abstract, mythical and fictional worlds of our minds. For example, as I have stated in one of my previous books, *Connections*, page 92, "I have no doubt that God exists, if nowhere else, then in the minds of billions of people." Only a dimwit could refute this.

It is certainly mindboggling that nonexistent concepts can be granted existence simply by imagining them. On the other hand, a closer examination of so-called nonexistent concepts is warranted, since there are exceptions. Take the abstracts zero and infinity as examples. Because of their nonexistence, even if we tried to imagine zero and infinity, we would find ourselves unable to do so. Nevertheless, when people think of zero, they imagine an oval symbol, but this is not zero, it is simply an oval symbol; or, people might imagine a dividing line between positive and negative numbers, but this, too, is not zero, it is simply a dividing line. Try as hard as you like, you will not be able to imagine zero – similarly, you cannot imagine infinity.

However, zero and infinity are the toughest abstract concepts to consider. A simpler concept is love; love is easy to imagine, except when it comes to loving one's enemy. We can point to Jesus Christ, of course, and prove how he loved his enemies on the cross of Golgotha, but what if the enemies were attacking lions or fatal viruses?

Loving your enemy may be easier when it comes to a nasty neighbor. I still remember a stubborn lady next door who insisted on me cutting down a tall spruce tree that grew on my lawn, because, she claimed, its shedding needles were ruining part of *her* lawn. The tree had been given to my oldest daughter by her school during her first school year. At first I refused to cut down the tree, but the woman behaved outright nastily toward my wife, and I had to try hard to see her viewpoint. Eventually, to keep the peace, I hired a tree cutter and paid him $500 to cut down and uproot the tree. Then, I spent another $500 to buy and plant three cedar trees where the spruce tree had spread out, and the neighbor lady came over, all smiles, and said, "Aren't these trees nicer than that ugly spruce tree?" I even agreed with her and felt good about having conquered my ill feelings toward her.

In another of my books, *Thoughts in a Maze*, page 30, I described how loving your enemy can make a friend of him. I'm convinced that serious attempts by us to love our enemies can have amazing effects, but does this also apply to threats like attacking lions and fatal viruses? We all know what our governments are doing to fight such viruses – they certainly do not love them! So, when trying to love our enemies, should we make distinctions? Are there relatively harmless enemies that we could easily love versus more harmful enemies that we should hate and even destroy? I wonder how Jesus Christ would have answered such questions.

There is certainly not much love lost between politicians – especially between politicians of different nations, sometime perceived, and treated like, enemies, even when grouped under one banner, such as the European Union. All throughout history, love in political arenas was short in supply; wars and royal murders can attest to this. During my 2015 summer visit to Germany, in the last week of June and first half of July, I had an excellent opportunity to follow the news of the love/hate relationships between the Greek Prime Minister Alexis Tsipras, German Chancellor

Angela Merkel, French President François Hollande, and other European leaders, negotiating another bailout for Greece. At the same time, our esteemed world powers, including the USA, the UK, China, Russia, France, and Germany, reached a nuclear agreement with Iran, which was not well received in the USA. There was not much doubt in my mind about the absence of love in the political arenas of the world at this time.

The sometimes positive but mostly negative effects of historical and modern political dealings and conflicts deserve much closer attention by us, and this was my endeavor for the topics of this book. After all, because of the still increasing spread of democracy around the world, ordinary people have much more power in the modern political arenas than ever before, and they should make good use of their power to curb the follies of politicians.

About the Author

Arthur O.R. Thormann has many interests:
Poetry, writing, reading, teaching, consulting,
photography, trusteeships, philosophy,
and software development, to name a few.
Germany is his country of birth; Canada is his
country of choice; Edmonton, Alberta,
is his hometown.